For Digs, Mr Magrath and Poppy

Nigel Slater is the author of a collection of bestselling cookery books, including the classics Real Fast Food, Real Cooking **and** Appetite. **He writes a much-loved weekly column in the** Observer **and has won six Glenfiddich awards for his writing and art direction. His beautifully written prose and unpretentious recipes have won him a great following. The** Sunday Times **says he is 'probably the best food writer around', whilst Arena describes him as a 'national treasure'.** Real Food **won the Glenfiddich award and became a number one bestseller.** Appetite **is the winner of the prestigious André Simon Award 2001.**

Angela Moore studied photography at Plymouth College of Art and design at Goldsmiths College, London. She has worked extensively for UK magazines including Rank, Maxim Fashion, Esquire, GQ, **and** Selfish. Rabbit **–her documentation of British greyhound tracks – has recently been exhibited at Browns, London.**

Nigel Slater
thirst

Introduction **I have always been a slave to juice, that sweet, heady nectar that dribbles from a ripe peach or melon, runs down your chin and drips on to your chest. Juice is what takes fruit from being simply a pleasure to a sensual** experience. All juice is good but some is sublime – consider mango, mulberry and papaya, cherry, peach and blackcurrant. I think of juice as the very essence, the succulence, of a fruit, and, much though I enjoy scrunching into the flesh of a ripe nectarine or squashing a raspberry against the roof of my mouth, it is the sweet juice rather than the texture of the fruit that really rings my bell. The cold liquor that drips from a perfectly ripe pear or a wedge of watermelon is, in my book, a gift from the gods.

Such pleasures are obvious to anyone who thinks of eating as a joy rather than 'something that just has to be done', but vegetables always remained for me the territory of the hardened juicer, the drink-yourself-younger sort of healthy-eating enthusiast. Fine, their world and welcome to it. That was until I first made a vast glass of carrot juice, a little tumbler of vivid beetroot, or added celery juice to apple to give it an even deeper flavour. Before I got a buzz from gulping down a glass of spinach and carrot or sipping a beaker of pear and watercress. Now, before you think I have lost the plot, or joined the world of people who eat for health rather than for pleasure, I should add that I have included no drink in this book purely because it is 'good for you' or gives you a buzz. Every drink is here because it tastes delicious.

Despite having owned a simple, cone-shaped citrus press for years, I resisted buying an electric juicer for the simple reason that I knew several people who had bought one, used it a couple of times, then put it away in a cupboard. Their excuse was always the same: they loved the juice but hated cleaning the machine. They have a point. But once I had swallowed the fact that cleaning the machine is part of the deal, I haven't stopped. Just as I have an espresso or two, a pot of yogurt, some greens and a salad every day; just as I have a slice of cake or an occasional sticky pudding, so I have a glass of juice. It has become as much a part of my day as a couple of glasses of wine with a meal.

No matter how crisp, luscious, soft or ripe the fruit or vegetables may be, for me it is the juice that is the crux of the matter.

'He who juices' **I have met people who are sceptical of the pleasure and power of fresh juice. I still encounter those who treat people-who-juice as being a bit cranky. At the very least, they think of us as being self-obsessed. I just don't get this. What, might I ask, is so weird about drinking** the freshly squeezed juice of a carrot that eating the vegetable itself is not?

The 'blame' for this lies perhaps with some of the more evangelistic juice books, whose authors claim just that little bit too much for their product – as if a glass of alfalfa juice was the panacea to all the world's ills. Even now, a fully paid-up member of the juicing world, I am still sceptical of some of the more outlandish claims and find an overdose of near-hysterical enthusiasm a difficult thing to digest.

Juice can be a powerhouse of vitamins and minerals that help to keep us in good health. It can keep our skin clear, our hair shiny, our cheeks glowing. Juice can rid us of the toxins of modern living, it can help with all manner of ills and fill us with vitality. But these are bonuses, and the point of pushing a fruit through a machine to extract its liquid will, for me, always be the pleasure of drinking the end product. The fact that it might, just might, cure everything from hiccups to PMT is a bonus, an extra, a glorious freebie.

The health thing

What we eat and drink affects our health. While the negative consequences of a regular diet of fried food, beer and ciggies build slowly over the years, the benefits of a glass of fruit or vegetable juice can be felt almost immediately. If you don't believe me, then push three fat, crisp carrots through the juicer, mix them with the freshly squeezed juice of two oranges or grapefruit and drink the result. Now tell me, honestly, that you don't feel more energetic, livelier and generally more 'healthy'. An instant up. A happy pill in a glass.

Few would deny that what we put in our mouths has some bearing on our well-being. Witness the short-term calming effect of letting a square of milk chocolate gradually dissolve in your mouth, or the uplifting quality of a bowl of hot, clear noodle soup with ginger and chilli. We don't need statistics here; the impact of food and drink is something we can feel for ourselves.

The fresh, clean taste of most juices is an instant clue to the effect they will have on our bodies if we let them become a regular part of our food and drink intake. Just as the bland, milky attributes of ice-cream, risotto or mashed potato will soothe us and the soft warmth of fresh bread or a newly baked bun will comfort, a glass of freshly squeezed juice will invigorate us like nothing else. Well, nothing else legal. Yet, and here is the rub, I eat and drink firstly for pleasure and only secondly for my long-term health. So you will find no cocktails of vodka, spinach and brewer's yeast here just because it might cure a flagging libido or athlete's foot. The point of this book is to pass on the pleasures to be had in extracting the juice, the nectar if you like, from fruits and vegetables. The bottom line is that the suggestions here are included only because I think they taste good.

More than juice

A quick glance through Thirst will tell you that my passion for juice is not just confined to drinking it neat. I also mix my juice with yogurt, with ice-cream and even sorbet. Once you do that, your juice needs another name, hence the plethora of smoothies, thickies and crushes. None of these names do I actually like (though they are far less cringe-making than some I have come across) but they are nevertheless necessary. And it goes without saying that a juicer is not vital to enjoy many of the drinks in this collection. Around half of them use a blender, albeit a decent one that will take the odd ice cube without choking to death, and in some cases you can even get away with just a citrus press.

The equipment

You can't juice without some sort of juice extractor. Unless, of course, you fancy grating every fruit then wrapping it in a clean towel and squeezing the life out of it. The juicer I use most is my little citrus press. It is not a designer number, just an old-fashioned stainless steel citrus press that cost about a fiver. I use it for halved oranges, lemons, grapefruit and the occasional lime and pomegranate. But then, that is all it is good for.

The extractor you choose will almost certainly depend on what you are prepared to pay. After a few false starts, I spent a small fortune on an American-made centrifugal machine that gets more juice out than the cheaper ones. You end up with more liquid for your money, a drier pulp and (wicked) you get filter papers that take away some (though not all) of the hell of cleaning it.

There are plenty of juicers on the market for around fifty quid. They are pretty good, though some seem to do the job better than others, by which I mean quieter, neater or generally more efficiently. I haven't named names here because a) unlike some cookery writers, I don't accept freebies in return for editorial mentions and b) the speed at which equipment changes means that today's best buy is tomorrow's also-ran.

Without getting even remotely technical, most juice extractors are what are called centrifugal juicers, which grate the fruit and vegetables and then whiz them in a steel drum to extract the juice. The pulp either collects on the inside of the drum or is thrown out into a pulp collector. Either way, it is a good thing for your compost heap. By all means start with a cheaper juicer in case you don't get into the habit, but give serious thought to one of the expensive jobbies. They will probably last for ever.

Cleaning the bloody thing

The world must be littered with unused juicers. For every one in daily use there must be three left on bottom shelves, tucked behind the pasta machine next to the ice-cream maker. There is a jolly good reason for this. Don't believe a word you read about how easy a juicer is to clean. None of them are. Though it must be said that some are easier than

others. In my experience, it goes something like this:

1 – **Remove the lid and get it to the sink without the debris that is stuck to it dropping off (you won't; it always falls off just as you reach the cooker hob).**

2 – **Unscrew the sticky knob holding the** grater blade in place. You may need **a tea towel to do this if it is slippery.**

3 – Lift out the grater blade and the **drum without trapped juice dribbling out. Slop bits of soggy pulp on the work counter and the floor.**

4 – If your machine has a filter paper, first try to find the top or bottom edge so that you can peel it away from the mesh while catching any loose juice dripping through the hole in the bottom on your way to the bin. Get filter paper out without it splitting and depositing pulp on the floor.

5 – **Hold filter basket under furiously running water. Furiously running water hits edge of basket and sprays water over**

sink, floor and your clothes.

6 – Scrub the blade without getting bits of scrubber stuck in the teeth. Grate knuckles on teeth.

7 – Wash the pouring spout, unwind the celery strings that have wrapped themselves around the knob that holds the blade on, and have another go at getting bits of apple and carrot out of the mesh basket. If you don't, they will only dry and you'll never get them out.

8 – Alternatively, forget about it for a day or two. Lift lid and find basket covered in fur and a deep smell of cider.

There is no way out of this. I remain convinced that it is the cleaning of the myriad parts of the juice extractor that stops the juicer becoming as much a part of our lives as a toaster or a kettle. The facts are simple. If we want fresh, life-enhancing juices, we must understand the first rule of juicing: cleaning the juicer is an unavoidable part of the deal. The bottom line is we must either wash up or shut up.

Getting the habit

With apologies to the much respected National Canine Defence League – a juicer is for life, not just for Christmas. How many of us take a juicer into our homes without thinking. Or give one as a gift? How many of us play with our new toy and promise to take it out every day, only to get bored with it the day after Boxing Day? A juicer is something that needs constant care and attention long after the novelty of its arrival has worn off. There are too many abandoned juicers. Rather than buying a new one, perhaps you might like to think of adopting one from a friend who cannot cope with theirs. That way, you will make them feel better about it and you will have given an abandoned juicer a new home.

The benefits of juiced fruit and vegetables can be felt almost instantly, but the real gains come only with regular drinking. It is just the same as going to the gym or swimming. You feel great after you have done it – though I reckon that at least some of the feel-good factor after I have been is pure, undiluted smugness – but the true benefit is felt only when you keep it up on a regular basis. The body is choc-a-bloc with toxins. One glass of juice a week is not going to shift that lot, in just the same way as a once-a-week work-out will make little difference to that belly.

The information In this book I set out a
                                number of suggestions
for juices you may like to try. Some are
stunning, others delicious and all are

good to drink. One or two are acquired tastes but they are all something I drink happily. You won't find many, if any, that make you shout 'Yuk!' and fling the glass down. You probably know I like my food too much for that.

After the suggestions, I tell you what to do with them. I do this not to state the obvious but because it is not always clear whether something should go in the juicer or the blender. I tell you when to peel and when something will taste better or be more beneficial with the skin left on. Though the main reason I tell you when to peel is that peeling a fruit just because you want a glass of juice is a bit of a pain, so the less often we have to do it the better.

How much liquor you get from a fruit or vegetable and, just as importantly, the quality of that liquor, will depend on a number of things: the variety and freshness of the produce; its ripeness; and the type of machine you are using. So you can take most of the 'Makes a large/medium/small glass' with a pinch of salt.

Ripeness

I have spent much time and anticipation assessing the perfect moment to eat a fruit, and now rarely make the mistake of cutting into a pineapple or a pear before it is truly, joyously ripe. But when juicing, things are rather more complicated. When you pick up a fruit to eat in the hand or toss into a fruit salad, ripeness is all. Yet when you push it through a juicer you will find excessive ripeness is not necessarily such a good thing. Try to juice a truly luscious, drippingly ripe pear and you will end up with pale brown slush. Strangely, it will appear many times sweeter than the whole fruit -- so sweet that it may be less refreshing than you had hoped.

A slightly crisper fruit will have a less honeyed sweetness to it and will give you more juice. This absolutely does not mean you should use unripe fruit, just that it need not be as sensuously ripe as if you were choosing a fruit to eat as a snack. And if you do find a melon, a fig, a pear, a peach that is at its peak, and it is as near perfection as you could ever hope for, then eat it as it is. Don't try and juice it.

Some Other Stuff **I don't juice for the health benefits that come with eating lots of fruits and vegetables. They are simply a bonus of the juicing process.** Here and there, I use a few terms that may need a bit of explanation. I'm being completely non-technical here. Remember, I'm not a nutritionist, but simply a guy who likes drinking juice.

Antioxidants **Here's a bundle of good news. Antioxidants are a group of nutrients found in fruit and vegetables and include vitamins C, E, A and beta-carotene. They get their name from the fact that they attack those oxygen molecules known as free radicals that damage healthy blood cells and can cause hardening of the arteries.** Beta-carotene **One could write pages about this stuff, and especially about its reputation as an anti-cancer nutrient. I could explain how it is a pigment found in certain fruits and vegetables, how the body converts it to vitamin A, and how it is found at its highest levels in vivid orange fruits and vegetables. But this is a book about**

pleasure, not another 'juices are good for you' book. So I shall simply say that beta-carotene is all of the above and can be found in heroic quantities in carrots, pumpkins, oranges, peaches, apricots, papayas, mangoes, passion fruit, sweet potatoes, Charentais melons, tomatoes, peppers, chillies, chard, Savoy cabbage, kale, spring greens and broccoli.

Vitamin C Most fruits are buzzing with the antioxidant vitamin C – especially citrus, kiwis, blackcurrants, strawberries and papaya. Helping to build strong teeth and bones and to heal wounds, it is available in abundance to anyone who juices regularly. You need about 60mg of vitamin C per day, more if you smoke or drink heavily, but just one average orange contains almost a day's requirements.

Vitamin A Essential for healthy vision and fighting infection, this vitamin is found mostly in animal and dairy products. However, I mention it here because the body is capable of converting carotene, and particularly beta-carotene – the pigment found in certain fruit and vegetables – into vitamin A. So one more reason for juicing red, orange and dark green fruit and vegetables.

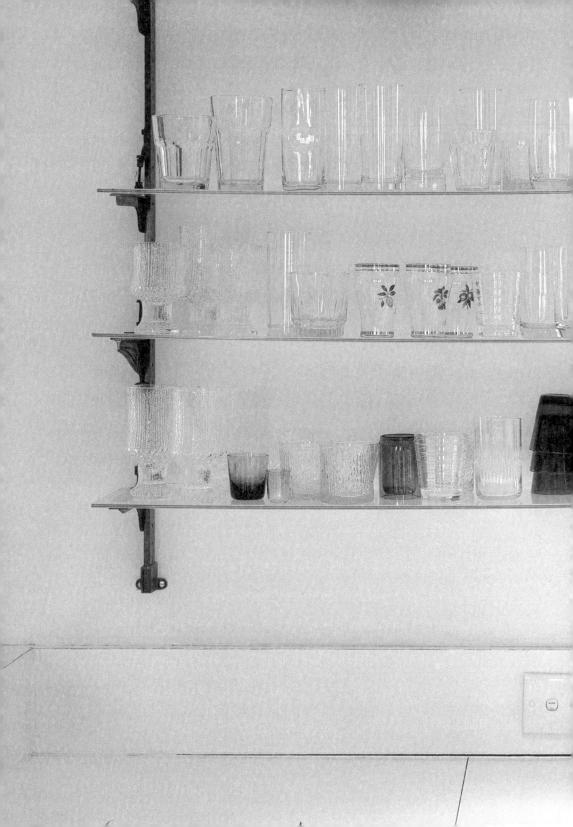

Contents

Melon
Watermelon Crush 41
Mango and Watermelon 42
Melon, Pineapple and Mint 43

Orange
Pure Orange Juice 44
Blood Orange Juice 45
Orange, Banana and Orange Blossom 46
Orange, Ginger and Mint 47
Orange and Lemon 48
Orange and Celery 49
Double Orange Smoothie 50

Papaya
Papaya and Lime Juice 51
Papaya and Grape 52
Carrot and Papaya 53

Passion Fruit
Passion Fruit, Orange and Lime 54
Passion Fruit Smoothie 55

Peach and Nectarine
Nectarine Yogurt Thickie 56
Nectarine Nectar 57
Peach and Strawberry 58
Peach, Raspberry and Redcurrant 59
Peach and Lemon Yogurt 60
Nectarine, Banana and Raspberry Smoothie 61

Pear
Pure Pear Juice 62
Pear and Blueberry 63
Pear, Lemon and Mint 64
Pear, Melon and Cucumber 65
Lettuce, Pear and Lime 66

Pineapple
Pineapple Mint Shake 67
Pineapple and Celery 68
Pineapple and Banana Smoothie 69
Pineapple and Mango Smoothie 70

Raspberry and Pineapple Smoothie 71

Raspberry
Pure Raspberry Juice 72
Raspberry and Orange Smoothie 73
Raspberry and Blood Orange 74
Raspberry Milk Shake 75
Raspberry Frozen Yogurt Shake 76
Pink Grapefruit and Raspberry Thickie 77
Blackberry, Raspberry and Redcurrant 78

Spinach
Spinach and Apple 79
Spinach and Carrot 80
Spinach, Carrot and Tomato 81

Strawberry
Strawberry and Orange Juice 82
Strawberry Milk Shake 83
Strawberry–Peach Frozen Yogurt Drink 84
Strawberry and Grapefruit 85
Apple and Strawberry 86

Tomato
Tomato and Carrot 87
Tomato, Celery, Parsley and Radish 88
Sunday Morning Tomato Crush 89

Indulgence
Iced Cappuccino 90
Iced Mocha 91
Double Chocolate Milk Shake 92
Real Hot Chocolate 93
Hot Mocha with Gingernuts 94
Blueberry Banana Smoothie 95
Passion Fruit Ice-Cream Smoothie 96
Clementine and Lemon Fizz 97
Bloody Mary 98

Sweet Apple and Orange
Raspberry and Apple
Apple and Blackcurrant
Hot Blackberry and Apple
Apple and Plum
Blueberry, Apple and Lemon
Apple **An unsung bonus of juicing is that**

flavours are often louder than in the whole fruit. The distinct characteristics of each variety of apple, say, are even more apparent in the juice than they are in an apple eaten in the hand. The nuances of mouth-puckering Bramley, warm, nutty Egremont Russet and light, sparkling Discovery are instantly recognizable when the fruit is crushed and sitting in your glass. On the downside, the dull, watery liquid that comes from those shiny imported red and green apples so beloved by greengrocers and supermarkets is even more noticeably insipid.

The range of apples available in farm shops and farmer's markets from late summer till Christmas is positively heartwarming. You can usually taste the apples before you buy; most stallholders carry a penknife. Each apple will give a markedly different juice. Here is a short list of apples worth looking out for and their distinctive characteristics:

Discovery **First of the season; light, sparkly, clean and mild, with a slight strawberry flavour.**

Blenheim Orange **Nutty, with a hint of fresh young hazelnuts; think of this as a sweet cooking apple. I have just planted one of these in my garden.** Orleans Reinette **Nutty and faintly spicy.** Egremont and other russets **Warm, intensely nutty, sometimes with a faint note of orange or spice.** Ellison's Orange **A faint note of aniseed to it, though not unpleasant.** Bramley, Howgate Wonder, Lord Derby **Vibrant, sharp and invigorating – will take some letting down with mineral water.** Royal Gala **Few apples are more depressing (save perhaps the Washington Red and Golden Delicious) but it is one of those varieties that has taken easily to organic production, so turns up with grim regularity in organic boxes during winter and summer, when there are few of our own about. You get masses of juice from it, and you can always perk up this sweet, dull liquid by adding half a peeled lime to the juicer. This will also stop the juice going brown.**

Apples need neither peeling nor coring before they meet up with the juicer but it is best to pull out the stalks. You will

need to slice them into segments to get them through the feeder but they are the least messy of all fruits to juice. The liquor oxidizes within minutes, so I squeeze a shot of lemon or orange in first, which seems to stop the discoloration without having much effect on the flavour. The crisper the apple, the clearer the juice. Floury, late-season fruit will produce a cloudy juice.

Apples are, along with carrots, one of the major cleansing juices, used in fasting and in detox diets. They are higher in vitamin C than they appear and also contain vitamins A and B. It is worth knowing that most of the vitamin A is in the skin. Packed with minerals such as copper, iron, potassium and phosphorus, the apple is a little powerhouse of goodness.

It is interesting that the pectin in apples has such a profound effect on our health. Without getting too yucky, let me tell you that it is good at absorbing toxins and helping them move quickly through the digestive tract. I know you really wanted to know that.

2 large, heavy oranges
5 medium-sized sweet apples
Sweet Apple and Orange
a gentle, early morning
winter juice.
Makes 2 large glasses

2 medium-sized sweet-sharp
apples, such as Granny Smith
or Worcester Pearmain
100g (a couple of large
handfuls) raspberries
Raspberry and Apple
Makes 1 medium to large glass

01

Adding a little orange to juice from a sweet apple such as Cox's Orange Pippin, Gala or Laxton's Fortune has the effect of intensifying rather than masking its flavour. It also stops the apple juice discolouring. The ensuing apricot-coloured froth that tops your juice is faintly reminiscent of baked apples filled with marmalade.

Either cut the oranges in half and squeeze them on a traditional citrus press or slice away their peel with a small knife and push them through the juicer.

Remove the stalks from the apples, cut each fruit into large segments and shove them into the juicer. The essential bit is to marry the two juices as quickly as possible to stop the apples oxidizing.

02

A sweet, refreshing juice for deepest summer. I ignore the fact that raspberries contain a small amount of saturated fat and concentrate instead on their high quantity of fibre and vitamin C. I have made this with imported winter raspberries and it was pretty good too, though a tad more expensive.

Twist off the apple stalks, then cut the fruit into large chunks. Push them, with the raspberries, through the juicer.

2 medium-sized sweet apples,
such as Cox's
75–100g (a couple of large
handfuls) fresh blackcurrants
Apple and Blackcurrant
Makes 1 medium to large glass

20 blackberries
2 apples
Hot Blackberry and Apple
Makes 1 large glass

03

Juices that pack a bit of a
kick are more refreshing
than the milder ones. The
amount of kick you get from
this one will depend on how
many blackcurrants you add.
The result is best taken over
ice cubes, in which case it
will look like a glass of
cloudy rosé spritzer. A light
juice that you can drink in
large quantities – if you can
be bothered to stalk all
those currants.

Remove the stalks from the
apples and slice them into
pieces that will fit your
juicer inlet. Pull the
blackcurrants from their
stalks. Push the apples and
currants through the juicer.

04

When fruit is cultivated, it
is almost always sweeter
than it is in the wild. This is
partly due to the tinkering
of plant breeders, who
assume that sweetness is
good, sharpness bad. Well,
you know I disagree with
that. I love fruit with a snap
of tartness, so whenever I
can I make this juice with
the wild blackberries that
poke through my fence from
next door. One of the very
few juices I ever warm up,
it is heavenly on a cold
autumn afternoon.

Push the blackberries
through the juicer with
slices of unpeeled, uncored
apple. Pour into a small,
stainless steel pan and heat
gently until hot, but stop
long before it boils. It will
taste and smell like
blackberry and apple pie.

8 small, sweet plums (or even greengages)
2 small apples, such as Discovery
Apple and Plum
Makes 1 small glass

2 medium-sized sweet apples
a few squeezes of lemon juice
a large cupped handful of blueberries
Blueberry, Apple and Lemon
Makes 1 large glass

05

Save this one for late July, August and September, when the farmer's markets are full of cheap plums and apples. It is not worth doing with expensive imported fruit. I initially made it with the first of the season's tart little Discovery apples and a batch of cheap and cheerful purple-red Czar plums. The result was a cleansing juice with a distinct autumnal back note to it. As the autumn progresses, try different varieties of apples and plums, culminating in the rather sticky but hugely enjoyable Cox's and Victoria. A sweet, almost honeyed juice.

Stone the plums, stalk and slice the apples and pulverize everything in the juicer. Your reward will be a glass of richly flavoured amber juice, which is high in both beta-carotene and vitamin C.

06

This dusty blue berry is a veritable powerhouse of good things. There are anthocyanins (the pigments that give the fruit its colour), which help protect against high cholesterol levels, and, according to The Juicing Bible by Pat Crocker and Susan Eagles (Robert Rose $10.95), this little round berry is also a source of natural aspirin. As if that wasn't enough, it is big-time on pectin, which is another stalwart of the anti-cholesterol brigade. I eat as many as I can while they are cheap, usually in midsummer. They can get very expensive during winter, which is bad news for someone like me, who thinks of them as a healthy version of M&Ms.

Pull the stalks from the apples and cut the fruit into thick slices. Squeeze a few squirts of lemon into a large glass. Push the apples and blueberries through the juicer into the glass.

Banana Smoothie
Banana, Honey and Vanilla
Banana and Orange Smoothie
Banana Ice-Cream Shake
Banana Lemon Smoothie
Strawberry Banana Smoothie

Banana **There is little or no juice in a banana. Yet it is a must-have in this book. I include it for the magical**

effect it has on yogurt drinks, giving body and a deep, velvety richness. As such, it is one of the most useful ingredients of all, almost turning a juice into a meal. To tell the truth, the thing I really like is the way banana drinks taste like those ice-creams you used to get as a kid but they don't seem to make any more.

The banana smoothie is a life-saver for anyone who finds themselves too busy to throw a meal together before they go out. I don't care how late you are, it takes less than a minute to zzzzzzz a banana or two, a splash of yogurt and any soft fruit you can find into a long, creamy, nutritious drink. It is worth remembering that a smoothie is faster food than a sandwich.

Bananas are full of fibre, high in calories and a good source of potassium and vitamin B6. They won't go through the juicer, so blender drinks only here. The rules for a banana smoothie are the same as for a banana cake: the riper the fruit, the deeper the flavour. You can use overripe fruit – no one will see the brown bits in a smoothie.

2 large ripe or overripe
bananas
250ml natural yogurt
an ice cube
Banana Smoothie
Makes 1 medium glass

To No. 07 add:
a vanilla pod
2 tablespoons thick or runny
honey
Banana, Honey and Vanilla
Makes 1 medium glass

07

If I am going out for one of
those evenings where there
is a chance I might end up
having more to drink than
to eat, this is what I drink
before I leave the house. It
stops the booze getting the
better of me (sometimes).

Peel the bananas, break
them into chunks and blitz
them in the blender with the
yogurt and ice. You will end
up with a mild and creamy
shake, good as it is, but even
better with a few simple
flavourings (see No. 08).

08

Much, much pleasure here.
A smooth, creamy and
nourishing smoothie that I
can drink all too much of. It
tastes like melted ice-cream.
The idea, by the way, came
from those genius guys who
make Innocent smoothies –
the ones I still buy even
though I make my own. I
think they put apple juice
in theirs, too.

Cut the pod in half crossways.
Save one half for your next
one. Slice the remaining
piece in half lengthways.
Using the point of a small
knife, scrape out the sticky
black seeds and add them,
with the honey, to the yogurt
and banana in the blender.

Blitz.

250ml thick natural yogurt
a large orange
3 medium-sized ripe bananas
Banana and Orange Smoothie
Makes 1 medium to large glass

3 ripe, very soft bananas
a little milk to blend
a small (100ml) tub of vanilla
ice-cream
Banana Ice-Cream Shake
Makes 2 medium-sized
glasses of heaven

09

**A mild, milky juice is
sometimes what I need first
thing on a Sunday morning.
Nothing cloys here. There
is an underlying freshness
from the orange that will
appeal to those who usually
find yogurt-based smoothies
on the rich side. This is not
exactly one to blow your
socks off.**

**Put the yogurt in a blender.
Halve and squeeze the
orange and add the juice to
the yogurt with the peeled
and broken bananas. Blitz
till smooth and milky. For
a thicker juice, add another
banana; for something more
quaffable, add some apple
juice or still mineral water.**

10

**This has to be the all-time-
great milk shake. The riper
the bananas, the better the
flavour. Black-skinned
bananas, the fruit inside
sticky and dark yellow,
make a sensational shake.
Do it.**

**Peel the bananas and break
them up, dropping them into
a blender. Pour in enough
milk to come half-way up
the bananas. Scoop in the
ice-cream and blitz till
smooth and creamy.**

2 medium-sized ripe bananas
100ml (that's about 2 big
balls) lemon sorbet
still mineral water
Banana Lemon Smoothie
Makes 2 medium glasses

6 strawberries
a banana
100ml plain, live yogurt
4 ice cubes
Strawberry Banana Smoothie

11

**Fab. A sweet-sharp,
refreshing drink with a
velvety, treacly texture. It
slithers down soothingly.
There is no dairy produce
in this, though there is, of
course, a bit of sugar. I have
recently found an organic
lemon sorbet, from Rocombe
Farm, made with spring
water and organic lemons,
which makes me feel a bit
better about the sugar.**

**Peel the bananas and put
them in a blender with the
sorbet and a few big
splashes of mineral water.
Blitz till thick and smooth.**

12

Absolute and utter bliss.

**Hull the berries, peel the
banana. Chuck everything
in the blender and errhm,
well........blend.**

Beetroot, Carrot and Orange
Beetroot, Celery, Apple and
Radish
A really good mixed
vegetable juice
Beetroot **Apart from the vampiric
undertones of drinking juice of
an almost arterial scarlet, it is the deep
earthiness of raw beetroot juice that can
be unnerving. Even with the fat, round
roots energetically scrubbed. I still find**

this rich juice has a distinct taste of garden soil.

Yet as juices go, it is one of the most cleansing, full of the beta-carotene that you would expect from a vegetable this colour, and a minor but easily assimilated source of iron. It is generally considered a juice to drink in small quantities.

Few juices make me feel quite so boosted and energetic, but what with its colour and its beefy, earthy thickness I find a full glass almost too much of a good thing. There is a way round this. The sharpness of citrus – grapefruit, orange and clementine – will cheerfully cancel out the more strident blood-and-earth tones. They also add a lightness and freshness to what is naturally one of the heavier juices. Fifty–fifty is a good start, but it is worth trying a bit more or less either way until you find something that suits your taste.

Expect vitamins C and B6, beta-carotene, folic acid and iron not to mention scarlet fingers and red spottles over the kitchen from scrubbing the beetroots.

2 large winter carrots
a small beetroot
2 blood oranges
Beetroot, Carrot and Orange
Makes 2 medium glasses

Deep claret-red juice for a winter's day. The sweetness of the carrot and citrus takes away the unnerving earthiness of the beets. Blood oranges are available from just before Christmas until April, and sometimes have a red blush to their skins. Of course, you can substitute the usuals if that is what you have. This looks more like a blood transfusion than a glass of juice. Be brave.

Give the carrots and beetroot a serious scrubbing, cut off any green stems and slice into pieces suitable for your juicer. Halve the oranges and squeeze them on a citrus press (I know, I know, two machines to clean, but this is the most time-smart way). Then pour the juice into a large glass. Place the glass under the juicer nozzle and push the carrots and beetroot through the machine. Do it this way so that the carrot juice falls directly into the orange juice, which will prevent it oxidizing quite so quickly.

a small beetroot
a medium-sized sweet apple,
such as Jonagold or James
Grieve
4–5 radishes
2 large stalks of celery
**Beetroot, Celery, Apple and
Radish**
Makes 1 medium glass

half a small beetroot
a medium-sized sweet apple
2 large stalks of celery
6 medium-sized chard leaves
or a handful of spinach leaves
**A really good mixed
vegetable juice**
Makes 1 large glass

14

**Sweet, gently earthy and
curiously creamy, this has
become one of the juices I
make most often. It is a bit of
a 'meal in a glass'. The radish
comes through loud and clear,
though not in a hot sense.**

**Cut the crown from the
beetroot and slice the
beetroot into pieces that
will go through the juicer.
Remove the stalk from the
apple and slice that too.
Top and tail the radishes.
Pulverise everything in the
juicer. You will get 2 large
glasses of deep red juice
with a pink, creamy head
like Guinness.**

15

**Mixed juices don't really do
it for me. I like flavours to
be loud and clear, not all
jumbled up together. This
one is different, though.
There is a distinct taste of
beetroot, but not so sweet
and heavy as when it is
juiced alone. The juice has a
milky taste to it, and a sweet
but patently earthy nose.
The spinach or chard is
packed with phytochemicals
and the celery and apple are
both high on the must-eat
list. The overall flavour is
mild and highly drinkable –
a good all-rounder in terms
of flavour and health.**

**Pulverize everything in the
juicer, pushing the chard or
spinach through alternately
with the other ingredients.**

Carrot **The sweetest vegetable juice of all. A powerhouse of minerals and vitamins. Just watching that vibrant liquid spurt glasswards from your juicer is surely enough to convince anyone that there is something in this juice lark. Well, it convinced me.**

Carrot is what I call a great base juice. It marries well with everything from mango to orange and offers welcome sweetness to bitter juices like watercress. There is

also the not insignificant point that, unlike so many other fruits and vegetables, it gives you a lot of juice for your money. Flavours worth trying with carrot are ginger, mango, beetroot, watercress, tomato, grapefruit, apple, pear and lime.

One large glass of carrot juice will boost your beta-carotene levels like little else. It also contains goodly amounts of vitamins A, B, C, D, E and K (vitamin K is the one that helps the blood coagulate), plus trace minerals by the score, including phosphorous and potassium. The big deal with this juice is its cleansing (for which read detox) effect on the liver. That means that this is the one to drink the morning after a few too many bevvies.

Carrot juice oxidizes almost quicker than any other. Once the colour has turned even slightly brown, there is no point in drinking it. Worse, this oxidization happens in seconds. The best way to stop it is to squeeze an orange or lemon into the glass first, so that the carrot juice falls directly into it.

a lime
5 or 6 medium-sized carrots
a knob of ginger the size of
your thumb
2 apples
Carrot, Apple, Ginger, Lime
Makes 1 large glass

an orange
4 medium-sized carrots
parsley – 3 or 4 good bushy
sprigs
Carrot and Parsley
Makes 1 medium glass

16

There is an almost sherbety quality to this foamy orange drink. It's sweet, it's creamy, it's frothy (and is beginning to sound like a Guinness), with a startling snap of heat in the background. A morning juice. With little to peel and nothing much to chop, this is one of those juices that require little more effort than the ability to lean on the plunger.

Roll the lime on the table with the palm of your hand. It will be juicier that way. Cut it in half and squeeze it into a very large glass. Shove the carrots through the juicer into the glass, peel the ginger and push that through too. Cut the apples up a bit, tug out the stalks and push them through. You will get a vast glass (actually enough for two) of creamy, glowing juice.

17

Why, I hear you ask. Well, I could say that parsley is very good for you (chlorophyll and trace elements) and that it is a first-class blood cleanser. But the truth is that I actually like the taste – as green as anything can taste, like pure, concentrated chlorophyll. But it does need mixing with the carrot, otherwise you're in for a nasty surprise. It is essential that the parsley is spanking fresh.

Squeeze the orange into a glass. Push the carrots through the juicer into the glass, at some point shoving the parsley through too.

an orange
a large mango, ripe, ripe, ripe
4 or 5 medium-sized carrots
Carrot and Mango
Makes 2 medium glasses

You need to use both the blender and the juicer for this – a drag – but it's a truly stonking juice so perhaps it doesn't matter. The colour is almost fluorescent, hardly surprising with all that beta-carotene in it. It is worth remembering that a mango used before it is really ripe is a wasted mango.

Cut the orange in half and squeeze it into the blender jug. I do this through my fingers so as to catch the pips. Peel the mango, hold it over the blender jug and slice away the flesh, letting it fall into the jug with any juice that drips and dribbles from it.

Push the carrots through the juicer. Tip the carrot juice in with the mango and orange and blend till smooth. It will be quite thick at this stage, so thin it down slightly with cold, still mineral water, but take care how much you add; even a little water will make a huge difference to the taste and texture.

Celery **As vegetables go, you get a lot of juice from a head of celery – but then we should expect that from something that so obviously has a high water content. I mean, there is so much** water in this stuff you can virtually see through it.

Once there was just white celery, made so by covering the stems to keep them white. Now we have green celery too, which to my taste seems more refreshing but less earthy. If I have a choice, I buy the white because I like that mineral hit, but the green is lusher and easier to get hold of. As a drink, celery has much going for it in terms of getting those minerals into our bloodstream, but it is a salty, faintly medicinal juice. Better, I think, to mix it with another. Consider it a base juice to which you can add other, more potent juices such as watercress, spinach or carrot. As such, it is unbeatable, having an earthy backnote that seems to temper any strident bitterness or overt sweetness.

The long, crisp ribs of celery contain small amounts of folic acid, sodium, potassium, vitamin C and the B vitamins. They juice like a dream. With the satisfying quantity of juice that comes out, there are few vegetables so pleasing to push through the funnel of a juicer.

4 stalks of celery
8 florets of broccoli, stalks
and all
2 pears

Celery, Broccoli and Pear
Makes 1 large glass

On paper, broccoli appears to be a perfect food. Certainly there is much to be gained in terms of vitamins and minerals: A and C, iron, folic acid, potassium, magnesium and zinc, plus fibre and phytochemicals by the bucketful. Pity, then, that it should be such a boring, mono-flavoured vegetable to eat. Unless of course you toss it in oyster sauce and garlic or smother it in a blanket of buttery Hollandaise sauce. However green and wholesome it may be, I am not sure anyone would want to tuck into a glass of broccoli juice. The 'nose' is distinctly cabbagy, the taste salty. But it does make an extraordinarily fine mixer – partly, I reckon, because the salt brings out the other flavours. I chucked the pears in here for some necessary sweetness.

Scrub the celery under running water, rinse the broccoli and quarter the pears, removing their stems – you can leave the cores and seeds in. Push everything through the juicer. What you will end up with is a neutral-tasting juice of the purest jade, fresh, green-tasting and very slightly salty. Pure, gentle, clean are the words that spring to mind as I drink this mild juice.

3 large, crunchy, juicy celery
stalks
about 30 small, seedless
green grapes
Celery and Grape
Makes 1 large glass

4 stalks of celery
4 medium to large carrots
Carrot and Celery
Makes 1 large glass

**From time to time you find
unlikely ingredients that
work together perfectly. At
first sight, there is no reason
why these ingredients should
work the way they do. Yet
think a bit further and what
you have is one ingredient
that is quite earthy and
salty, and a second that is
refreshing and sweet. It
works, and produces a well-
balanced, mild juice. Gentle,
cooling, cleansing.**

**Make sure the ingredients
are chilled, then force
through a juicer.**

**Carrot juice is too sweet for
some people. The salty kick
of celery will take the
sugary edge off just enough
to make a glass of carrot juice
strangely refreshing.**

**Push everything through the
juicer and drink immediately,
before it has time to discolour.**

4 stalks of celery
6 tomatoes, not overripe
a large apple
Celery, Tomato and Apple
Makes 1 medium to large glass

1/2 green melon
a lime
3 bushy sprigs of mint
2 large stalks of celery
Celery, Mint, Melon and Lime
Makes 1 very large glass

22

One of the most gratifying things to come out of my juice obsession has been the mixed juices – the 'cocktails', if you like. When you get them right they are as satisfying as a meal. Get them wrong and they taste like compost. This one provides not a meal (by any stretch of the imagination) but a clean, light-tasting alternative to the salty, tomatoey gloop of commercial juices. It has a freshness to it that bottled vegetable juices lack.

Shove everything through the juicer bar the apple stalk. What you will get is a light, faintly murky juice that makes you feel good. Though it is hardly what you might call sexy.

23

Long, cool, minty, refreshing. This is the juice that I want first thing in the morning, even before I get out of bed.

Remove the seeds from the melon. (I have a silly but satisfying habit of trying to see if I can get them all out with one scoop of the fingers. There's usually a couple left behind.) Cut the peel from the lime with a small, very sharp knife. Push everything through the juicer. You will get a very large glass of pale, jade-coloured juice that will wake you up, but rather soothingly.

Pure Cherry Juice
Cherry and Apple
Cherry and Apricot

Cherry For serious juicers only, this one.
It will take you longer to stone
the cherries than it will to juice the
fruit and drink the result. But that result
is a juice of intense, almost wine-like
flavours and deep, but not cloying,
sweetness. The colour is majestic. First-
time cherry crushers might like to try it
just as it is – you won't get much juice for
your money and effort – but after that
first, concentrated shot of blood-red
nectar you might be happier to use it as

a mixer. The potent cherry flavour comes through even when you mix it with citrus, though its zenith seems to be reached with apples and pears. A truly sublime juice.

The darker the cherry, the higher the amount of beta-carotene. And it is beta-carotene we want for its anti-oxidizing properties. The natural plant chemicals in cherries are thought to help fight cancer, and of course there is a fair amount of vitamin C.

No domestic juicer I have yet met can cope with cherry stones. If one accidentally gets in it sounds like a scene from 'The Texas Chainsaw Massacre'. Pit the fruit over a bowl to catch all of the treasured juice. You can slit each cherry then pop out the pit, or use an olive stoner (or that peculiar bit with the hole in the handle of some garlic presses). If you have a lot to do, you can get quite a speed up with an olive stoner. Remove the stalks too, as you need to for any fruit. Expect much of the juice to end up over your fingers and table, and bear in mind that it stains as badly as beetroot.

Pure Cherry Juice

24

Deep garnet and richly bright, pure cherry juice is the juicer's equivalent of a bottle of claret (unless cherries are at the peak of their season, the price won't be much different either). I have, just twice, served this in small Moroccan tea glasses after dinner. I am sure everyone thought it was a liqueur. Yes, it's as special as that.

Stalk and stone the cherries. Have patience, the end result is worth it. Now push the lot through the juicer. Serve in shot glasses.

2 large handfuls of cherries
a large, sharp apple
Cherry and Apple
Makes 1 medium glass

around 250g cherries
8 not-too-ripe apricots
Cherry and Apricot

25

One of the best. I first tried this in an attempt to eke out a meagre amount of rather expensive early season cherries, which was when I first found out how clearly the intensity of cherry juice comes through in a mixed juice. Later, I spotted this mixture in other books. I reckon you need two big handfuls of cherries per apple. You get a drink that is distinctly cherry but also has a welcome snap of acidity from the apple. As the fruits come through the blender, you get a rather lurid red and green froth, but it dies down and the juice is a sensation.

Stalk and pit the cherries. Remove the stalk from the apple, then cut the fruit into thick slices. Push through the juicer with the cherries.

26

The late-season apricots coincide with the cherry glut. We are talking serious amounts of beta-carotene here – so, on the remotest chance that you are not overwhelmed by the ruby-streaked, Greek-sunset iridescence and the sweet, almost floral flavours, just think of antioxidants. It makes sense, of course – this combination of fruits works superbly in a fruit salad too.

Pit the cherries and apricots and push them all through the juicer. If you have a juicer with a filter paper, then I suggest you remove it for this one. You will curse me when you come to wash up but the juice will be richer for it. This is one of those purée-like juices that need serving in small amounts, with a splash of mineral water to take it to drinking consistency. It is essential that the ingredients are cold, so refrigerate them before you juice.

Pink Grapefruit, Orange
and Pineapple
Grapefruit, Carrot and Apple
Mango and Grapefruit
Grapefruit and Passion Fruit
Grapefruit and Beetroot

Grapefruit **White, pink or ruby.
A grapefruit for everyone.
The darker the flesh, the sweeter the
juice. Even then, it's one to make you
shudder. I sometimes think that this is
my favourite juice of all, with its clean,
bright taste and copious yield. Sharp,
though, even the red stuff.**

**The classic white fruits with their pale
yellow flesh offer dazzling tartness
somewhere between a lemon and a
Valencia orange. An antidote to the
general sweetness that pervades our food
nowadays. A serious wake-up call.**

**Pink and ruby grapefruit are a more
recent introduction – OK, over ten years**

now – but easily outsell the original white fruits. The juice is sweeter, the colours stunning – like sherbet sweets – and the extra fructose makes them easier to drink in quantity. But beware, they still pack a punch, and too much can upset your stomach. (If you are on prescribed medicines, check with your doctor before chucking back a whole glass; it can be contraindicated with certain drugs.) Me, I just can't get enough. I love the way you only need a couple of big ones to fill an entire glass.

The darker the flesh, the more beta-carotene your grapefruit contains and therefore more of those precious antioxidants, including vitamin C. If you peel-n-juice rather than cut-n-squeeze you will also take in the pith, which contains pectin (which moves everything through the gut a bit quicker) and even more of those antioxidants. There are small amounts of B vitamins in there as well, and a small but nevertheless interesting collection of minerals – potassium, magnesium, phosphorus. All good stuff, but the real buzz is the one you get from the startling and copious juice.

3 small to medium oranges
a pink grapefruit
1/4 large pineapple

Pink Grapefruit, Orange and Pineapple

Makes 2 very large glasses

a grapefruit
3 medium-sized carrots
an apple

Grapefruit, Carrot and Apple

Makes 1 large, refreshing and invigorating drink

27

If ever you meet someone who doesn't believe in the power of juice to make you feel great, give them a glass of this. It's like drinking pure sunshine. The three flavours work together to give a drink that is both sweet and sharp, smells fresh and clean and is light on the stomach. This is my favourite morning juice, especially in the depths of winter. If you try only one juice in this book, make this the one.

Cut the oranges and grapefruit in half and squeeze them on a citrus press. Pour the juice into your blender. Trim the peel from the pineapple and cut the flesh into chunks, removing any very tough core. Blitz everything to a smooth, foaming orange drink.

28

A mixed fruit and vegetable juice that is actually pleasant to drink (and there aren't many of them).

Slice the peel from the grapefruit – which colour you have matters little – then chop the flesh and put it though the juicer with the carrots and apple (core, pips and all, but remove the stalk).

a medium-sized ripe mango
2 grapefruit
a few ice cubes or still
mineral water
Mango and Grapefruit
Makes 1 large glass

1 large grapefruit
4 passion fruit
Grapefruit and Passion Fruit
Makes 1 medium glass

29

In a way, this seems to be even more successful than mango and orange, probably because the extra citric acid in the grapefruit accentuates the flavour of the mango (as, incidentally, does a shot of lime juice). You need a couple of grapefruit per mango, otherwise the drink will be too thick. Even then, you can let it down with still mineral water.

Peel the mango and slice the fruit from the stone. I do this straight into the blender. Halve the grapefruit and squeeze them, adding their juice and the ice cubes or mineral water to the mango. Blend till smooth.

30

A real wake-up call. There is a sharp, slightly thin quality to white grapefruit juice. You can add a deep, fruity warmth to it by blending in the flesh and seeds of a passion fruit or two. Depending on how you feel about seeds, you might like to push the passion fruit pulp through a tea strainer first, or you can just blitz the fruit juice, passion fruit pulp and seeds in the blender till it is as smooth as you can get it. Even without a blender, you can make this juice. Squeeze the grapefruit over a citrus press, then cut the passion fruit in half, squeeze them into the fruit juice and pour through a tea strainer to extract the seeds. I rather like the dull crunch of the little seeds and often drink it as it is, seeds and all. Reckon on four wrinkled but heavy passion fruit per large grapefruit.

2 small, but not baby, beetroot
2 pink grapefruit
Grapefruit and Beetroot
Makes 2 large glasses

Anyone who finds the earthiness of beetroot juice just too much to handle will welcome the tart intrusion of a shot of grapefruit. The addition of citrus also socks a load of vitamin C into the beetroot juice for those who take an interest in such things. I find this one of the most energizing of all drinks, but it is not for the faint-hearted.

Scrub the beetroot clean and cut them into big chunks. Peel the grapefruit, then push everything through the juicer. As you drink down the bright magenta liquor, you can almost feel it rushing through your bloodstream.

Mandarins and Stuff

Clementine, Strawberry and Banana Smoothie
Tangerine and Mango
Mandarin and Papaya

The smaller citrus fruits – mandarin, tangerine, satsuma, minneola and clementine – have a subtly different flavour from the large 'China' orange. More rounded and infinitely sweeter. Part of their joy is that they peel so readily you can wolf them like sweets, but these fruits also have a juice that is copious in quantity and richly sweet in flavour. For once, you get a lot for your money.

They will (I guess) supply you with the same levels of vitamin C and bioflavonoids as the larger fruit. The flavour is defined enough to be mixed with even quite strong notes of pineapple and mango and yet still be recognizable. The firm, tighter-skinned tangerines and mandarins seem to have a deeper flavour than the loose-peeled 'baggy' satsuma. This is the juice for those who find the usual orange a bit on the acid side.

In the course of writing this book, I have had one or two real wake-up calls, and none greater than the glass of pure mandarin juice I had one November morning. It took half a bag of mandarins and produced one of the most vibrant drinks I have ever put to my lips. It reeked of Christmas. Interestingly, the same thing made with satsumas – the loose-skinned version of the mandarin – produced a less than joyful glass. You could, effectively, try all the fruits as they come into season. One of these, at least, is the juice I want to drink by the jugful on winter Sunday mornings, as I sit reading the paper, the pale morning sun streaming through the kitchen windows.

6-8 tangerines or other small
citrus fruits
a small, ripe mango
Tangerine and Mango
Makes 2 large glasses

a papaya
a small banana or half a big one
4 ice cubes
6 mandarins or other small
oranges
Mandarin and Papaya
Makes 2 large glasses

33

The mango flesh makes this
a thick, velvety juice, sweet,
luscious and emphatically
sexy. It is one of those juices
that make you feel as if you
have just spent an hour at
the gym. And if you have
spent an hour at the gym
too, then you should be
feeling unbearably healthy
and, if it were me, more than
a wee bit smug.

Cut the tangerines in half
and twist them on the cone
of a juice squeezer. Peel the
mango, cut the flesh from the
stone and blitz it in a blender
with the tangerine juice.

34

The eye-opening, lip-
smacking citrus juices are
all very well but sometimes
I want fruit that soothes
instead. This is one of those
gentle juices, a step behind
the usual dazzle of citrus
drinks. A calming winter
juice, and quietly satisfying.
Perhaps best drunk on a
morning that follows some
sort of overindulgence.

Peel the papaya, cut it in half
and scoop out and discard
the black seeds. Roughly
chop the flesh and put it into
a blender along with the
peeled and broken banana,
the ice cubes and the juice of
the mandarins. Blend till
smooth and bright orange.

Mango Orange Smoothie
Pure Mango Juice
Mango, Ginger and Grapefruit
Slush
Mango and Lemon Freeze
Nectarine and Mango Smoothie
Mango, Raspberry and Lime

Mango **A luscious, velvety juice, best sucked directly from a drippingly ripe fruit. Preferably whilst you are naked. Even better if you are not alone.**

With a mango, ripeness is all. Colour and size are no guide, though (a green mango can be as perfectly ripe as one the colour of an autumn sunset), so look instead for a bead of nectar at the stalk, occasional black freckles and a honeyed scent. Check your mango for ripeness by squeezing it firmly but respectfully with your whole hand. Don't poke at it with your thumb. Because if it isn't ripe yet, you will have just bruised it. The fruit should be heavy. Prime time is May, when the kidney-shaped yellow Alphonse variety comes in from India, which is when I buy them by the box from Indian grocers. Look out, too, for the small Thai mangoes in late winter. For the rest of the year, Jamaica, Peru, Brazil and Africa turn up with the goods.

Golden flesh, nectar for juice. This should be enough. Yet mangoes are high in beta-carotene and a good source of vitamins E, A and C. And, what is more, you get the stone to suck.

Mangoes have an affinity with dairy produce – think mango fool and mango lassi – but go easy adding the yogurt, as the rich, smooth flavour is easily overpowered.

Peeled mango discolours quickly, so stop the oxidization process with citrus juice. Lemon or orange will work well enough, but a lime, which grows in the same neck of the woods as a mango, is more appropriate. Few flavours flatter one another so generously. And don't forget to check the ripeness of each fruit carefully. A misjudged mango is a wasted mango.

a large, obscenely ripe mango
2 medium or 1 very
large orange
200ml (maximum) natural
yogurt
a squeeze of lime juice
Mango Orange Smoothie
Makes 2 medium glasses

Pure Mango Juice
A glass of pure sunshine

Mild, velvety, soothing – like melted ice-cream. Bad news: both blender and citrus squeezer to clean.

Peel the skin away from the mango with a small knife, then slice the flesh from the stone into the blender. Suck any remaining flesh from the stone – a perk, a small one, but none the less glorious.

Cut the oranges in half and squeeze them, pour the juice into the blender, tip in the yogurt, then blitz till thick, smooth and creamy. Squeeze a little lime juice into each glass.

Peel your fruit with a small knife, then cut off slices of the ripe, yellowy-apricot flesh. I do this over the blender jug so as not to lose one drop of the precious nectar. Blitz to a thick slush, then thin it down with chilled still mineral water and ice cubes. A shot of lime will accentuate the fruit's flavour.

half a ripe mango
the juice of 2 pink grapefruit
a slice of ginger about the size
of a pound coin
2 or 3 ice cubes
still mineral water

**Mango, Ginger and
Grapefruit Slush**
Makes 1 large glass

The term 'ginger up' is not without substance. The volatile oils in the fresh root dilate our blood vessels, thus improving our circulation. Whatever, ginger makes me horny. This thick and luscious drink is not especially thirst-quenching but it will invigorate, stimulate and warm us. It does have quite a kick though, as you might expect from a mixture of ginger and citrus.

Good news: beta-carotene, vitamin C, volatile oils such as zingiberene.

Peel the mango and slice the flesh into a blender, catching the escaping juice as best you can. A really ripe mango, heavy with juice, may well dribble down your sleeves.

Cut the grapefruit in half and squeeze them on a citrus press. Pour the juice into the blender. Peel the slice of ginger, cut it into thin strips and add to the blender. Chuck in the ice. Blitz, adding still mineral water if you prefer a thinner juice.

a small, ripe mango
the juice of half a lemon
2 balls of frozen yogurt
still mineral water

Mango and Lemon Freeze
Makes enough for 2

a ripe nectarine
a small, ripe mango
a scoop of lemon sorbet
still mineral water

**Nectarine and Mango
Smoothie**
Makes 1 large glass

**Thick, fruity and fluffy. You
will need a spoon here, so
you could argue against its
appearance in a book called
Thirst, but this cross
between a drink and an ice
is, after all, thirst-quenching.
Something for a scorching
summer's day with
Wimbledon on the box.**

**Peel the mango and slice the
flesh from the stone. Do it
over a blender so you don't
lose any of the precious
golden juice. Add the lemon
juice, the frozen yogurt and
a few splashes of mineral
water. Whiz till smooth
and thick.**

**Cool, mild and thick. A drink
for sunbathers.**

**Halve the nectarine and
discard the stone. Peel the
mango and cut the flesh from
the stone. Put the fruit in a
blender with the sorbet and a
few splashes of mineral water.**

Blitz.

half a large, ripe mango
a couple of handfuls of
raspberries – about 20 large
ones
the juice of a lime
4 ice cubes
still mineral water

Mango, Raspberry and Lime
Makes 2 medium to large
glasses

A slightly spooky texture to this, but it slips down easily enough. The flavours of both fruits sing loud and clear. With masses of vitamin C, beta-carotene and fibre, this is the juice to drink when you feel a cold coming or when you feel in need of an 'inner spring clean'.

Peel the mango and cut the flesh from the stone, dropping the flesh into a blender. Add the raspberries, lime and ice and whiz to a smooth purée, thinning with mineral water as you go.

Melon

Fragrant, sweet and refreshing. Melons produce copious juice in shades of amber, jade, gold and vermilion. **A ripe melon,** bursting with **juice, its flesh sweet as** honey **and soft as jelly,** seems too good **to reduce to a mere glass of coloured water.** When a **melon is at** its most luscious, I would **discourage you from juicing** it, suggesting **instead that you eat it as it is,** letting the **sticky juice** run **down your chin.**

When a melon refuses to ripen satisfyingly or when you have a chunk of watermelon in hand in midsummer, then I would thoroughly recommend pushing it through a juicer. You will get lots of juice and it will be sweet and creamy tasting. One of my favourite ways with melon is to take a watermelon, pick out the seeds as best I can, cut off the peel, and blitz the scarlet flesh in a blender with ice cubes. The result is a

vivid red, **hugely** refreshing drink. A breakfast juice of the first order.

If the melon has thin, crisp skin, like a Charentais or watermelon, then you need **not peel it before juicing. Soft or** bendy **skins such as those on some** Ogen **and** honeydews just c**log the juice**r. In Juicing for Health (Thorsons, £7.99), Caroline Wheater **points out that** melon **goes through the digestive sy**s**tem faster than any other fruit and so** restricts **the absorption of** other **fruits it** may be **mixed with.** An invaluable piece of **advice. So watermelon juice** should only **be drunk on its own. No hard**ship there.

Orange-fleshed melons such as Charentais and Ogen contain more beta-carotene than yellow-and green-fleshed fruit such as Honeydew. They are generally a bit sweeter, too. They are neutral and cooling to the body. There are reasonable amounts of vitamins A and C in melons but most experts seem to get more excited about the amount of adenosine – an anticoagulant that helps thin the blood. All I really care about is their honey-like sweetness.

a thick slice of watermelon
a coin of ginger, finely grated
4 ice cubes
still mineral water
Watermelon Crush
Makes 1 large glass

a 450g lump of watermelon
a very ripe medium-sized
mango
Mango and Watermelon
Makes 1 very large glass

41

A cool, dynamically refreshing drink for a hot summer's day. Like diving head first into a cold swimming-pool.

Cut the flesh from the watermelon and poke out the seeds. You don't have to be too thorough. Just do it till you get bored. Now chop the flesh up a bit and blitz it in a blender with the grated ginger, the ice cubes and a few splashes of water to help the blades engage. Result: one large glass of brilliant carmine slush – fabulous.

42

This looks like a slightly fizzy Heinz tomato soup. Sweet and hugely refreshing, it is packed to the gills with beta-carotene and vitamins A and C, and there's some folic acid and a few B vitamins in there too.

Cut the watermelon into pieces that will go through your juicer. There is no need to peel away the thick green skin or pick out the pips. Press it through the juicer; you will get a very large glass of pink juice. Peel the mango and cut the flesh from the stone, letting it fall, along with any escaping juice, into a blender. Tip the melon liquor in with the mango and blitz to a glossy, orange-scarlet juice.

Pour over ice.

half a small green melon,
ripe but not overripe
half a small to medium
pineapple
a small bunch of mint leaves
(about 20)
Melon, Pineapple and Mint
Makes 2 large glasses

43

**Frothy, refreshing, sweet,
with a crisp, fresh smell to
it, this is one of those
drinks I can't get enough of.
On the healthy side it has all
the cleansing properties
associated with melon plus a
rich cocktail of minerals and
enzymes from the pineapple:
vis-à-vis calcium, potassium
and folic acid. But the real
benefit is the cool, clear,
sweet juice. Litres of it.**

**Unless the skin of the melon
is very tough you should cut
it off with a large knife. Soft
melon skin just clogs the
juicer. Removing the skin
gives a more concentrated
juice. Discard the seeds.**

**Peel the pineapple and cut
it into large pieces. Feed the
peeled pineapple, mint and
melon into the juicer. You
will get a couple of large
glasses of clear, pale green
nectar with a mound of froth
on top.**

Serve over ice.

Pure Orange Juice
Blood Orange Juice
Orange, Banana and Orange
Blossom
Orange, Ginger and Mint
Orange and Lemon
Orange and Celery
Double Orange Smoothie

Orange I suppose I have always taken
the orange and its juice for
granted. I mean, have you ever, ever seen
a greengrocer's shop, street barrow or
supermarket without oranges? But it
takes on another dimension if you see
the apricot-coloured fruit on the tree at
the same time as its exquisitely scented

white blossom and you care to remember that it was originally brought from China by the Arabs as an exotic and fragrant treasure. They called it narandj.

You will get all the juice from an orange by simply cutting it in half and sucking. Then, if you are like me, you will tug the flesh from the skin with your teeth whilst turning the skin inside out at the same time.

To drink from a glass rather than the fruit itself, just squeeze the halved fruit on a citrus press. But. You will get more antioxidants from your orange if you can bear to peel off the skin but leave the white pith under it in place and then push the fruit through a juicer. You won't honestly get any more juice from your fruit, but what you do get will be better for you. It won't, though, taste much different.

All orange juice is high in antioxidants and vitamin C. Those who know their stuff reckon this juice is a 'total cancer-fighting package'. Oranges work brilliantly with carrot, strawberry, grapefruit and papaya.

Pure Orange Juice
Clean, bright, vital

Blood Orange Juice

For my money, there is no finer orange juice than that from a winter Tarocco orange. Orange-pink rather than vampiric magenta, it has a smack of sharpness to it that makes it more refreshing than the ruby-fleshed fruit. They can be the size of a small grapefruit, so a couple will be enough for a morning glass. This is the juice for a crisp, frosty winter's day. The colour, incidentally, is simply a freak pigmentation that apparently first happened in seventeenth-century Sicily and for which we are now asked to pay a premium.

The flavour of your juice will depend almost entirely on the time of year. Oranges are always in season but varieties come and go like any other fruit. It is just that we don't notice it quite so much as, unlike apples or figs, most oranges look pretty much the same.

Pure orange juice is best in the winter when we have the long-season Valencia, those heavy, juice-swollen fruits from Spain, and the Israeli Shamouti.

Organically grown oranges are now virtually the same price as the sprayed varieties. Look for heavy fruit with tight skin – a sign that it has been picked recently and is bursting with juice. If they still have their leaves, then even better.

The smaller ruby fruit that are sold in nets in the supermarket are sweeter than a standard orange, and have purplish-red juice. Their place of origin will depend on the time of year. It takes a good four or five to get a decent glassful but they can have a mellow, almost raspberry-like flavour to them. This one feels better for you as you drink it. It's all in the head, of course.

3 medium-sized oranges
2 bananas
orange blossom water

Orange, Banana and Orange Blossom
Makes 1 large glass

a walnut-sized knob of ginger
3 or 4 medium-sized oranges
6–8 large mint leaves

Orange, Ginger and Mint
Makes 1 medium glass

A fragrant juice. Halve the oranges and squeeze them on a citrus press. Peel the bananas and stuff them into the blender with the orange juice. Add a teaspoon of orange blossom water, or more, to taste, and blitz until smooth.

Peel and grate the ginger. Catch any juice – it will only be a pittance but will have much flavour (and the goodness of zingiberene). Squeeze the oranges, pour the juice into a blender and scrape in the ginger mush. Then throw in the mint leaves and blitz thoroughly.

2 or 3 fat, sweet oranges
a thin-skinned lemon
Orange and Lemon
Makes 1 medium glass

4 decent-sized oranges
4 small stalks of celery
Orange and Celery
Makes 2 medium glasses

The saltiness of the celery brings out the flavour of the orange, and you get your folic acid and a handful of B vitamins, too. Not the most visually ravishing of juices (it looks like the washing-up water after baked beans on toast) but its citrus-mineral overtones make up for it. Cleansing, invigorating and faintly earthy.

Peel the fruits, leaving some of the pith in place. Push the flesh through the juicer. You can, of course, simply cut the fruit in half and squeeze it on a citrus press – it saves washing up the wretched juicer but deprives you of the good stuff contained in the white pith.

What you get is about the brightest-tasting juice of all. Vivid and crisp. Brace yourself.

Peel the oranges and push them through the juicer with the celery stalks.

Serve over ice.

a medium glass of orange juice
a ball of orange or lemon sorbet
Double Orange Smoothie

**A heavenly, deeply flavoured
juice – pity about the sugar in
the sorbet.**

**Whiz the juice and sorbet in
the blender, briefly, just so
that the juice thickens.**

Papaya and Lime Juice
Papaya and Grape
Carrot and Papaya

A ripe papaya is one of the most fragrant fruits on earth. Its flesh is deep amber-orange, almost as soft and fragile as jelly. The ones we get in the West are generally pear-shaped and pale yellow and, it has to be said, not as heavily fragrant as those in the Far East (I have seen ones in Thailand the size of a small baby).

Ripeness is all. **A papaya is ready when it gives under a little pressure and feels tender at the thin end. Squeeze, don't poke. Your judgement of its ripeness is crucial. An unripe papaya tastes like marrow.**

Costing around a pound each, they seem expensive to end up as juice, but the flesh is thick and will take a bit of diluting with ice cubes or chilled mineral water, and you get a reasonable amount for your money. The flavour and colour of a glass of crushed papaya will remind you of holidays in the Far East, where it invariably turns up in long, tall glasses for breakfast.

When ripe, the flesh is pale orange, so you can expect a bit of beta-carotene here. It also contains the enzyme papain, which is supremely good for the digestive system (and means the juice works well as a marinade for tough meat, breaking it down to tenderness in record time). There have been claims about papain's ability to stave off wrinkles. A claim I am happy to go along with.

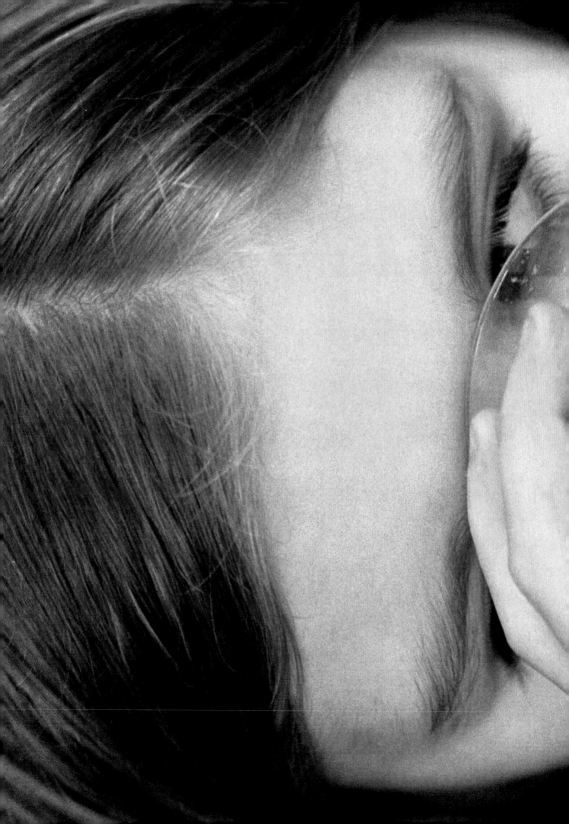

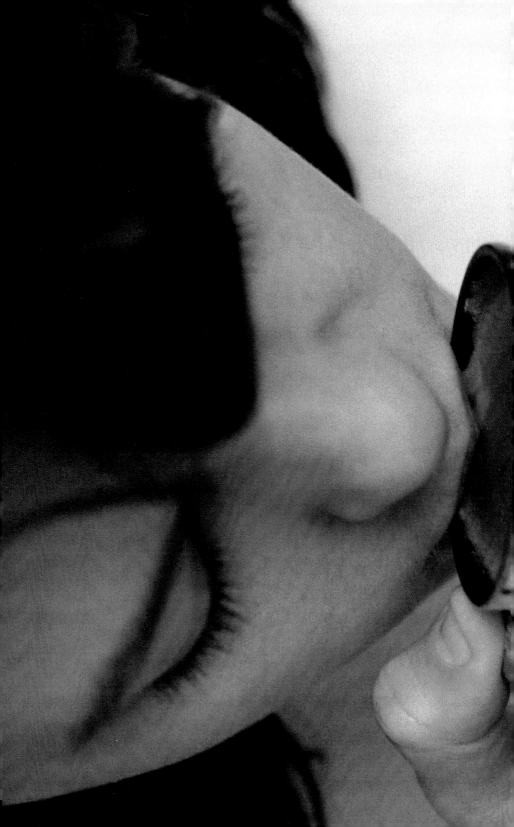

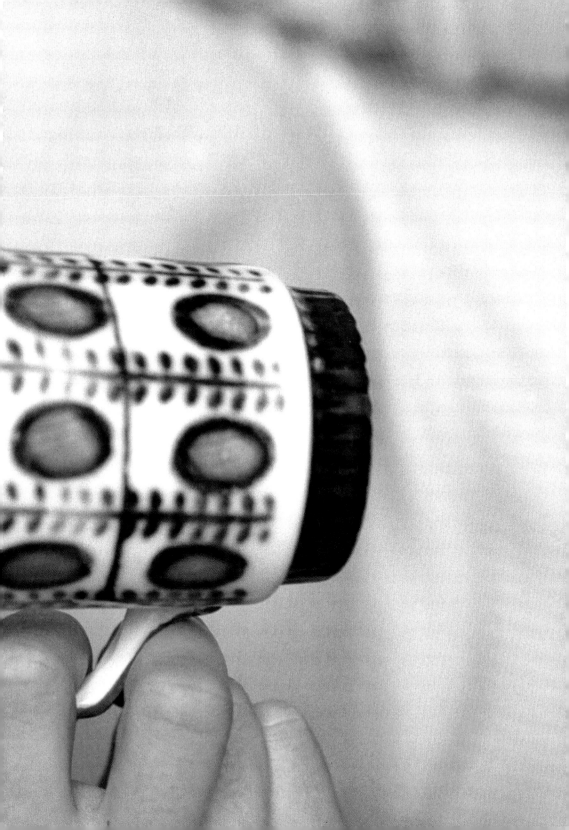

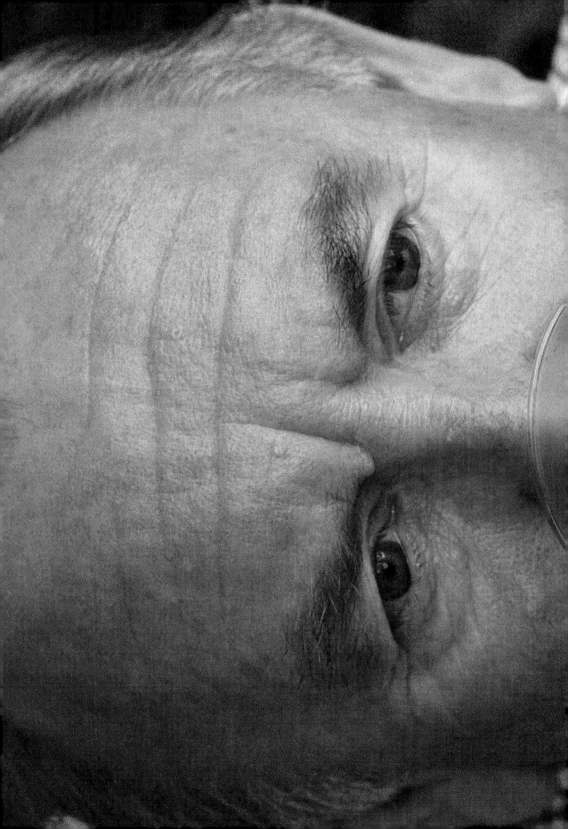

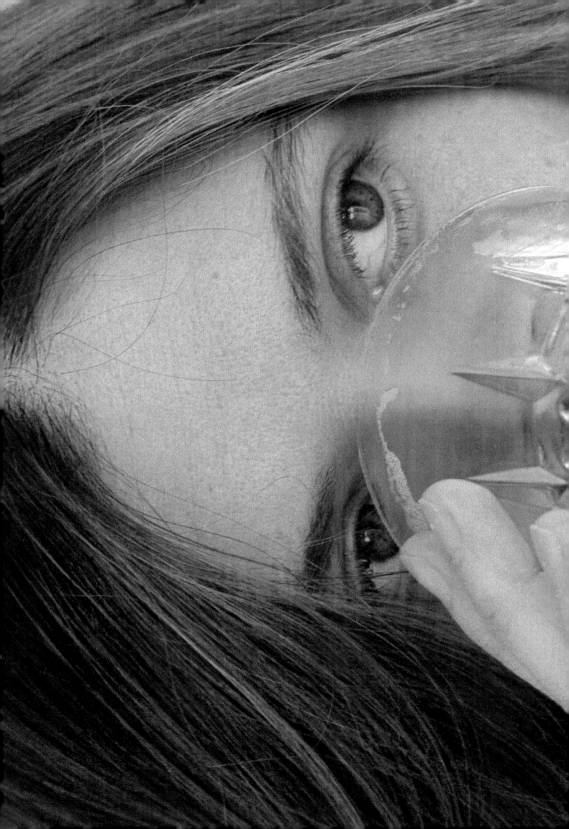

a ripe papaya
a small orange (not a
mandarin)
a lime
3 ice cubes
Papaya and Lime Juice
Makes 1 medium glass

a ripe, medium-sized papaya
about 30 small, seedless
green grapes
4 ice cubes
still mineral water
Papaya and Grape
Makes 2 medium to large
glasses

51

A glass of vivid orange
heaven. Few drinks are as
pure and clean-tasting as
papaya juice mixed with
crushed ice and a squirt of
lime to make its flavour
sing that bit louder. A glass
full of blue skies and long,
sandy beaches.

Slice the papaya in half along
its length. Using a teaspoon
or your finger (I use that
finger), scrape out all the
seeds and discard them. Now
carefully scrape the orange
flesh from the skin and let it
fall into a blender. Roll the
lime on the table, pressing
down on it with your palm –
this will soften it and
persuade it to give up more
of its juice – then cut it in
half and squeeze it into the
papaya. Add the juice of the
orange, the ice cubes, and, if
needs be, a little mineral
water. Whiz until thick and
smooth. It will be the colour
of an autumn sunset.

52

As a rule, I don't like clashes
of culture on my plate, and
the idea of grapes and a
tropical fruit may jar. Yet
they work here. As juice goes,
this is pretty much heaven
in a glass. The colour is that
of an Indian sunset, the
flavour mild and soothing,
the nose deeply fragrant.
Grapes are no longer the
expensive luxury they once
were and, like apples, they
are good for diluting
stronger juices without
altering the flavour too much.
As always, make certain your
papaya is truly ripe.

Halve and seed the papaya
and scoop the flesh into a
blender. Push the grapes
through a juicer and pour
the thin, green liquid into
the blender. Chuck in the ice
and some splashes of
mineral water and blitz to a
smooth, pinky-orange drink.

3 medium-sized carrots
a squeeze of lime juice
a ripe papaya
3 ice cubes
Carrot and Papaya
Makes 1 large glass

I am not a fan of those fruit and vegetable mixtures that contain half a dozen different ingredients all fighting to get control. To my tastebuds (and they are pretty good tastebuds), a simple mixture of only a couple of fruits and vegetables works better. The result seems bright and clear rather than muddled. Carrot and papaya, weird as it sounds, is one of those f and v mixtures that works brilliantly. And don't think I am trying to eke out the expensive flesh of a tropical fruit with some cheap root veg here. I include this mixture for its flavour – a mild, earthy fruitiness – and for the fact that it is one of the more drinkable examples of a fruit and vegetable juice. The colour alone will make you feel a couple of years younger.

Scrub the carrots, cut them up a bit and shove them through the juicer. Add a squeeze of lime to halt their oxidization and their inevitable discolouring. Halve and seed the papaya, scrape the flesh from the skin and purée it in a blender, pouring in the carrot juice and ice cubes.

Passion Fruit

Passion Fruit, Orange and Lime

Passion Fruit Smoothie

Sometimes, when the sky (or my mood) is particularly grey, I take a passion fruit, cut it in half and take a long, deep sniff. I am not sure there is a more uplifting scent. At least, nothing I can think of that carries with it such promise of brighter days to come. More often than not, I just suck the flesh out and crunch the seeds with my teeth.

Anyone new to this fruit may find it a bit of an oddity at first. Though most of the fruits you see in the shops are smooth and deep purple-black, a passion fruit is not really ripe and ready to cut until it is heavily pitted, almost wrinkled. That said, each fruit must weigh heavy in the hand to show it is full of juice. Light fruits tend to be dried out.

Despite a healthy crunch of fibre, this is not a fruit bursting with health-giving vitamins, apart from vitamin C. Neither is its interior awash with juice. The point of the passion fruit lies in the intensity of its flavour. Even a small amount (and that is all you'll get) is enough to boost a glass of orange juice or some yogurt. Lime, and indeed sharp yogurt, will lift its flavour even higher. The taste is sharp and warm and the texture that of scrunchy seeds held in a soft jelly.

To extract the juice from a passion fruit, you need to cut the fruit in half and scoop out the seeds and jelly. If you are not using the seeds – they tend to grind to grit in the blender – then scoop the entire contents into a tea strainer or small sieve balanced over a glass or cup. Push the flesh and juice through with the back of a spoon and discard the seeds. Alternatively, get rid of them later, pouring the finished drink through the sieve instead. Oh, and don't even think of trying them through the juicer; you'll lose the lot.

3 oranges
a lime
3 passion fruit
**Passion Fruit, Orange and
Lime**
Makes 1 medium glass

There can't be much wrong
with a drink the colour of
custard. Especially one that
is seriously packed with
vitamin C. This is one of the
best winter juices, bringing
with it the bright flavours
of citrus and tropical fruit.
You don't need an electric
juicer for this one, or for the
one that follows. This one
manages to be smooth and
sharp at the same time and,
if you whiz it for long enough,
doesn't need sieving either.

Halve the oranges and lime
and squeeze them, then pour
the juice into a blender. Cut
the passion fruit in half and
scoop the seeds, juice and
flesh into the citrus juice.
Whiz till smooth and deep,
creamy yellow.

4 passion fruit
a small banana
the juice of an orange
5 tablespoons natural yogurt
Passion Fruit Smoothie
Makes 1 medium to large glass

I hate the word smoothie but no other word so appropriately conveys the creamy, silky quality of this drink. Even the relatively small amount of passion fruit gives it a pronounced passion fruit flavour, though it doesn't overwhelm you. If you don't like the idea of sieving out the seeds from the finished smoothie – it is rather frustrating when you are thirsty – then sieve them out before you start with the help of a tea strainer and a teaspoon instead. If you like this one, you'd better check out the rather decadent passion fruit drink in the Indulgence section (No. 96).

Cut the passion fruit in half and scoop out the seeds, juice and flesh into a blender. Add the peeled banana, the orange juice and the yogurt. Blitz. The scrunched seeds need to be sieved out – I do this by balancing a tea strainer over the glass and pouring the smoothie through it with the help of a teaspoon. If the seeds don't bother you, then fine; they won't harm you and there is no need to sieve.

Peach and Nectarine

Please, please, don't juice a perfect peach. You will lose the touch of that velvet skin and soft flesh in hues of saffron and crimson, heavy with sweet juice. Bite into it, in all its luscious glory, and let its juices drip off your chin and down between your fingers. That is juice as good as it gets.

Anything slightly less than perfect, by which I mean the very good, the OK and the could-be-better, can go into the blender. Hard, unripe or squashy fruit won't do you any favours. There is not much reason for putting a peach through a juicer; you will only end up with a blob of rather beautiful slush. Better to blend this one.

The world seems to be split between those who prefer the soft, sexy fuzz of the peach and those who would rather bite into a

smooth-skinned nectarine. I am a peach man, but I do understand the pleasures of the latter, and when a nectarine is truly ripe and dripping with juice there are few finer fruits. Peaches and nectarines can be bought more or less all year in the supermarkets but I have yet to find a really great peach other than at the height of summer. The ones that land here in the winter are usually like tennis balls and rarely ripen properly. Those sensationally juicy fruits from France and Italy are usually here by late May and continue right through until October.

Not for nothing do we associate peaches with cream. Dairy produce works well with this fruit. Cream, yogurt and mascarpone all have something of an affinity here. Shakes, thickies and smoothies are pretty much the only way to go.

As a health note, yellow peaches are rich in beta-carotene (the white ones less so), vitamin C, folic acid, calcium and phosphorus. But who really cares when they produce a juice that tastes like heaven itself?

2 large, very ripe nectarines
100–150ml natural yogurt
the juice of half a lemon or less
Nectarine Yogurt Thickie
Makes 1 medium to large glass

2 large oranges
2 ripe nectarines
(or, of course, peaches)
3 ice cubes
Nectarine Nectar
Makes 2 medium glasses

A soothing, creamy thickie for a summer's morning. Like melted ice-cream. Pretty, too, with its crimson freckles. I sometimes put an ice cube in here as well, which makes a slightly thinner, more thirst-quenching drink. Of course you can do this drink with peaches, too. Whatever you use, there is no need to peel the fruit; that way, you get lots of crimson-coloured flecks through your thickie.

Halve the nectarines and remove and discard the stones. Slice the fruit into a blender, then add the yogurt and lemon juice. Blitz thoroughly – it takes a bit longer than usual because of the thick skin.

Given ripe, scarlet nectarines and decent oranges, this is one of my favourite drinks in the book. The very essence of summer. The colour, by the way, is stunning – brilliant amber-orange with flecks of vermilion.

Squeeze the juice from the oranges. Stone the nectarines and slice them into a blender. Add the orange juice and ice and blitz.

a large, ripe peach
a small orange
a handful of strawberries
4 ice cubes
Peach and Strawberry
Makes 1 large glass

a large, ripe peach or nectarine
a handful of raspberries –
about 20 or so
the berries from 5 or 6
sprigs of redcurrants
3 ice cubes
**Peach, Raspberry and
Redcurrant**
Makes 2 medium to large
glasses

**A thick drink of the purest,
clearest peach flavour. A
great colour, too – orange with
freckles of carmine. Serve
on a summer's morning.**

**Stone the peach and tweak
out the little twig of a stalk
if there is one. Slice the
peach into a blender, squeeze
the orange and pour the juice
on top of the peach. Add the
berries, halving and stalking
them as you go. Add the
ice cubes.**

Blitz.

**Sweet, but with a bit of a
punch, this one gets more
lively the more redcurrants
you put in. The redcurrant
season is July and August,
but you can get imported
ones several weeks earlier
and up to Christmas.**

**Halve the peach, pull out the
stone and slice the flesh into
a blender. Blitz with the
other fruits and the ice cubes.
You may need a splash of
still mineral water to make
it whiz round. Add more of
either of the red fruits to
make it sweeter or sharper.**

2 very ripe peaches
100ml natural yogurt
the juice of half a lemon
Peach and Lemon Yogurt
Makes 1 large glass

large, ripe nectarine
a handful of raspberries
a banana
3 ice cubes
still mineral water
**Nectarine, Banana and
Raspberry Smoothie**
Makes 2 medium to large
glasses

Smooth, creamy and apricot-coloured. This is the drink to make if you have truly ripe peaches or nectarines. A summer's afternoon drink that can be made without a juicer – you just throw everything in the blender. Choose a yogurt that isn't too thick, and add an ice cube or two to the blender if you want something more thirst quenching.

Halve the peaches and stone them. Blitz them in a blender – not a juicer – with the yogurt and lemon juice. Result – a rich, pale-orange thickie.

A real depth-of-summer drink, thick and cool. This is the sort of drink, both refreshing and sustaining, that I make when I come back from my daily swim. The colour of a Greek sunset, it becomes especially valuable when you realize that it is a quickly thrown-together juice involving little or no prep. Unless, of course, you are the sort of person who counts peeling a banana.

Stone the nectarine and slice it into a blender. Add the raspberries and the peeled, broken-up banana. Chuck in the ice cubes and whiz to a thick slush with a few splashes of mineral water.

Pure Pear Juice
Pear and Blueberry
Pear, Lemon and Mint
Pear, Melon and Cucumber
Lettuce, Pear and Lime

Pear **Elegant, gentle, suave. A juice to sip. When you want to eat a pear as dessert, you need to cosset it a little, watching it for a day or two until at last it reaches its peak of perfect ripeness. You will cradle it and give it a light, respectful squeeze to check its progress.**

At last, a day or two after you expected, it will be ready. That perfect point of ripeness will depend on how you like your pear to be, but in my book it should be almost the texture of sorbet.

Juicing is another matter. A ripe fruit, fragrant and tender, will give you nothing more than a sad little puddle of grey slush. Pears for juicing need to have a bit of a crunch about them – not hard, but quite a way from perfect ripeness. Then you get liquid rather than baby food. Remove the stalk but leave the core and pips in, then cut into pieces small enough to go into the juicer.

The variety of pear will, of course, affect the flavour of the finished juice, but the difference will not be as pronounced as that between varieties of apple. Even so, you can expect much rounded sweetness from Comice, a clean, delicate edge to Conference and very little flavour indeed from those imported winter pears from the southern hemisphere. Start looking for locally grown ones in late August – early September. They will be around until Christmas.

Pure Pear Juice
A gentle one

200g blueberries
2 not overly ripe pears
Pear and Blueberry
Makes 1 medium glass

Once in a while, I want a little glass of juice that is delicate, elegant, calming. This is for those moments. Pear and blueberry is the sort of drink that would probably feel more comfortable in a wine glass than a tumbler. A pale rosé in colour, and quite sweet too, a light, easily digested juice, perhaps the thing for a hangover or when you've been poorly. Only attempt this one when blueberries are at a reasonable price.

Whether you blitz Comice, Williams or Conference, you will get a small glass of delicately flavoured and rather beautiful juice that is the very essence of pear. It will taste even more pear-like than a pear. Strange but true. It might seem odd to suggest mixing it but the flavour is surprisingly deep and can be used to soften bitter tastes such as watercress or spinach. Mixed with berries, it produces a drink almost Edwardian in its elegance.

Shove the berries through the juicer with the sliced pears. Drink immediately; this one discolours. A squeeze of lemon or, better still, lime will slice some of the sweetness and stop it browning.

3 large, not overripe pears
half a lemon
8-10 mint leaves, fewer if you
are using a blender rather
than a juicer
Pear, Lemon and Mint
Makes 1 small glass

the flesh of one small, green
Ogen melon
2 flavoursome pears, stalks
removed
half a cucumber
Pear, Melon and Cucumber
Makes 2 large glasses

**A winter juice. Mild, clean
and fresh-tasting.**

**Cut the pears into large
pieces, remove and discard
the stalks. Squeeze the
lemon into a glass, then push
the pear and mint through
the juicer. If your juicer
won't have anything to do
with the mint (some just
gobble it up and no flavour
comes from it), then tip the
juice and some fresh mint
into the jug of a blender and
blitz it. Remember, though,
that no juice oxidizes and
discolours quicker than pear.**

Joanna Blythman, author of
The Food Our Children Eat
**(Fourth Estate, £7.99), told
me about this juice. As she
says, 'This combination is
perfect. It looks marvellous:
dense, pea-green juice, which
separates out to form a milk-
shake-type foam on top. The
cucumber gives it a stunningly
fresh nose, without being at all
aggressive. It tastes positively
creamy although it contains
no dairy products. Best of all,
it feels filling, even though
its calorie count is negligible.'**

**Pulverize everything in the
juicer. If you haven't got a
juicer, give the whole lot a
long whiz in a blender or
food processor. The mixture
will be soupier and less
elegant but it still tastes fine.**

8-10 medium-sized lettuce
leaves with crisp stems
half a lime
2 pears – not too ripe
Lettuce, Pear and Lime
Makes 1 medium glass

**It takes a while to get used
to swallowing things that
are green and frothy, but
some of the best drinks look
like something the Addams
family might make for
breakfast. Lettuce is a juice
that needs mixing. The
bland taste of the whole leaf
becomes dramatically bitter
when juiced; it needs a
sweet partner. But it adds
a unique flavour and is both
cleansing and refreshing.
Surprisingly, it is rich in
calcium and beta-carotene.
Lettuce works well with
pear, which adds the
necessary sweetness
without overpowering. An
addition of lime lifts it into
a quietly pleasing juice.**

**Wash the lettuce thoroughly,
unless you like the idea of
the odd slug or aphid in your
juice, then push it through
the juicer, stalk ends first,
together with the peeled half
lime and the pears (cut up
and stalks removed). The
result will be a mildly
uplifting, frothy-top juice of
a rather beautiful jade green.**

Pineapple The pale, honey-scented nectar you can extract from a peeled pineapple makes me long to move to a warmer climate, where such a glassful of juice costs pennies rather than pounds. Few drinks (the exception is mango) so successfully bring the sun flooding into your day. I know this juice best from holidays – in particular, ones to Thailand and Mauritius, where it turns up in large, chilled glasses every morning. Mix it with orange juice or, better still, clementine and really make it sing.

A whole pineapple will make a lot of juice, but you can happily put half back in the fridge for tomorrow. The flavour is deep and will take a little thinning down with mineral water, if you want. If you have no juicer, peel the pineapple, whiz it in a blender, then cut it with mineral water. You may find that a slightly unripe pineapple – in this instance – produces more juice than one heavy with liquid. There is a bonus too of potassium, vitamin C, beta-carotene and, in small amounts, several of the B vitamins.

You do, rather boringly, need to peel this fruit before you juice it. A drag. But then it hardly takes more than five minutes. Lop off the crown first, rest the fruit flat on the chopping board and slice down the outside with a serrated knife. The little brown dimples matter very little in the juicer, so don't bother trying to winkle them out.

Like apple, grape and carrot, pineapple is a good mixer and has enough clout to stand up to other fruits and vegetables. Even so, you will have to go a long way before you find a more welcome sight than a jug of pure pineapple juice on a winter's morning.

half a medium-sized
pineapple
200ml natural yogurt
6-8 large mint leaves
a little still mineral water
Pineapple Mint Shake
Makes 2 large glasses

a small – though not
miniature – pineapple
4-6 medium-sized stalks of
celery
Pineapple and Celery
Makes 1 large glass

67

A clean-tasting juice for the morning. I like these light-on-the-tummy shakes to start the day; they are like being gently shaken awake. This is one of the best hangover cures imaginable, giving you a clear head but also being easy on the gut.

Peel the pineapple and cut the flesh into chunks. Tip them into a blender with the yogurt, mint leaves and a little mineral water. The amount of water you add will ultimately depend on how thick you want your shake to be. Blitz in the blender until smooth and bubbly.

68

The lush sweetness of ripe pineapple responds very well to the faint saltiness of celery. The flavours flatter one another, the celery bringing a bucketload of minerals with it, including potassium, sodium, phosphorus and calcium. As a whole, the juice is refreshing, mild and gentle. Nothing to shock the system here.

Peel the pineapple and cut it into large chunks, then feed them into the juicer. Wash the celery and poke most of it through (there is something strangely pleasing about pushing celery down the funnel of a juicer). Taste as you go. Stop when things are tasting good. You can tweak the sweet or salty notes to suit your mood.

a quarter of a pineapple
a large banana
4 ice cubes
the juice of a large orange

Pineapple and Banana
Smoothie
Makes 1 medium to large glass

the flesh from half a large,
ripe mango
a quarter of a large, ripe
pineapple
a small knob of ginger
a little still mineral water or
3 or 4 ice cubes

Pineapple and Mango
Smoothie
Makes 1 large glass

A smooth, rather laidback juice. Mild, silky and golden and packed with beta-carotene and vitamin C. I sometimes make a jug of this on a Sunday afternoon in the middle of winter when we are sitting watching a daft old film. For that you will need a whole large pineapple and a couple of big mangoes.

Put the mango flesh into a blender. Peel the pineapple, cut it into large chunks and add to the mango. Peel the ginger and grate it into the fruit. You don't have to use all the ginger; just a little will make a difference. Blitz thoroughly with the water or ice cubes until smooth and creamy.

The creamiest juice, all fluffed up like a melted marshmallow. Little would anyone know it's just fruit and ice cubes. The ice is essential, by the way.

Peel the pineapple and the banana, then put the roughly chopped flesh into a blender. Blitz with the ice cubes and orange juice until cool, pale and frothy.

a quarter of a large pineapple
the juice of a large orange
ice cubes
2 handfuls of raspberries

Raspberry and Pineapple Smoothie

Makes 1 medium to large glass

Sweet-sharp, bright-tasting, fuschia-coloured juice for any time of year. Imported or even frozen raspberries will work well here. Even so, trying this juice out one March afternoon went a bit against the grain. I like to respect the fact that some things are meant to go together and, according to my rules, raspberries and pineapples shouldn't because they come from entirely different cultures. One sip of this brilliant red juice and my principles went out of the window.

Peel the pineapple, cut it into chunks and whiz it in a blender with the orange juice, ice cubes and raspberries.

Pure Raspberry Juice
Raspberry and Orange
Smoothie
Raspberry and Blood Orange
Raspberry Milk Shake
Raspberry Frozen Yogurt
Shake
Pink Grapefruit and
Raspberry Thickie
Blackberry, Raspberry and
Redcurrant

Raspberry

You get very little juice from a raspberry but what you do get is intense, vivid crimson with a sharp, rich flavour. Few juices are quite so potent in terms of concentrated flavour, which makes this a good juice for mixing with other, lighter and bulkier ones such as orange or apple. You will need some other fruit to push through the juicer at the same time. Otherwise, you will just end up with expensive, though utterly beautiful, carmine slush.

The hundreds of seeds in every raspberry are a good source of fibre.

Raspberries also contain vitamin C plus traces of iron, potassium and niacin. The seeds are apt to block the juicer filter, so patience is needed to let all the juice run through. You need a lot of raspberries to make a decent amount of juice, but it is worth remembering that their flavour goes a long way. Shoved in the blender instead of the juicer, they will make a seedy purée, which can be let down with still mineral water.

Varieties to keep an eye out for are Leo, Malling Jewel and Glen Arran. Late in the summer and early autumn, try Autumn Bliss; there are few more sumptuous, deep-flavoured raspberries. From July to October they are cheap enough but once the home-grown supply is over then the imports will come up a little more expensive. They are not to be sniffed at, though, offering surprisingly good flavour (for a little berry that has come half-way across the world) and often a heady fragrance, too. I am not fond of fruit out of season but, come those long, dark February days, a punnet of imported berries will often find its way into my shopping bag.

Pure Raspberry Juice

250g raspberries
a large orange
250ml natural yogurt
6 mint leaves

Raspberry and Orange Smoothie
Makes 2 medium glasses

Raspberries have an affinity with dairy produce – think of fool, ice-cream and pavlova. It therefore makes sense to use them in a smoothie, whizzed up into a creamy drink with yogurt. The colour is something you can't get away from. Even a few berries will send your smoothie a deep, bubblegum pink.

Rinse the raspberries and tip them into a blender. Halve and squeeze the orange and add the juice to the berries, then spoon in the yogurt and add the mint leaves.

Blitz till smooth.

A glass of pure, undiluted raspberry juice? You must have either money to burn or a vast source of free berries. That said, a shot glass of the vivid scarlet juice – like the glowing red of a stained-glass window – is a glorious thing to behold. Do it just once, perhaps with the late-season raspberries that turn up in September.

2 blood oranges
250g raspberries
3 or 4 ice cubes and a little
still mineral water to dilute
if necessary
Raspberry and Blood Orange
Makes 1 medium glass

In the grey depths of winter, when the only locally grown fruit available are pears and apples, I do turn to the odd punnet of imported berries. Their vibrancy is uplifting. Though I have never quite worked out how a packet of raspberries can come all the way from the southern hemisphere in fine condition yet can't make it from the local shops to my kitchen without turning to jam.

Oranges have long worked with raspberries, and none better than the deep-red blood oranges we get in winter. I refuse to call them ruby or blush oranges, or whatever new name some namby-pamby supermarket consultant has dreamed up. To me they are simply blood oranges, packed with sweet, garnet-coloured juice.

Peel the oranges with a small knife, then push large chunks of the fruit through the juicer with the raspberries and ice cubes. You will get a glass of glowing red juice, and the flavour will be deep enough for you to add a little mineral water should you wish.

a small tub (100ml) of very
good vanilla ice-cream
125g punnet of raspberries
still mineral water
Raspberry Milk Shake
Makes 2 medium glasses

**Raspberry Frozen Yogurt
Shake**

**I have fond memories of an
ice-cream called Raspberry
Ripple (long gone, like Fab,
Zoom and old-fashioned
choc-ices). This shake
reminds me of those long,
hot summers, when I seemed
to have an ice-cream
permanently in my hand.**

**Let the ice-cream soften
slightly, then put it into a
blender with the raspberries
and enough mineral water to
help the blades engage. This
shouldn't be more than a few
glugs from the Evian bottle.**

**Same thing as above but
with plain frozen yogurt
instead of ice-cream. It
doesn't matter if you can
only get strawberry flavour;
in fact, it's probably just as
good. If you put these two
side by side, you will be hard
pushed to tell the difference.
A luscious shake which, for
those who are interested, is
very low in fat.**

2 large handfuls of
raspberries
a large banana
juice of a pink grapefruit
**Pink Grapefruit and
Raspberry Thickie**
Makes 2 largish glasses

20 blackberries
20 raspberries
the berries from 5 stalks of
redcurrants
3 ice cubes
**Blackberry, Raspberry and
Redcurrant**
Makes 2 medium glasses

77

A wake-up call, yes. But also
a really power-packed drink
that can double as breakfast
(thanks to the banana). The
grapefruit adds a real buzz
and the whole package is
light but sustaining. You'll
probably need to chuck in a
couple of ice cubes to thin it
down and make it longer and
even cooler. A good one to give
to people who are sceptical
about the joy of juice.

Put the raspberries in a
blender with the peeled
banana and the juice of the
grapefruit. Blitz. If it seems
too thick, add a little water or
a couple of ice cubes. Sieve it
to get out the raspberry seeds
if you must, but I rather like
the velvety, seedy texture of
this one. Just the thing for a
summer's morning.

78

Anything this colour – a deep
black-red – is bound to be
life-enhancing. Perhaps not
surprisingly, it is also a
seriously cleansing drink.
Must be all those seeds.
Should you ever come across
any loganberries or tayberries,
use them instead, and you
can change the redcurrants
for black ones, too. The point
is to end up with a dark,
richly flavoured berry drink
with massive amounts of
vitamin C and fibre. Pitched
against this, a cold doesn't
stand a chance.

Blitz in a blender. Sieve if
you can't handle the seeds.

Spinach and Apple
Spinach and Carrot
Spinach, Carrot and Tomato

Spinach **I sipped my first glass of spinach juice with trepidation. I knew I liked the vegetable, but that was when the leaves were lightly cooked to an emerald green and smeared with melted butter. Eating a frothing green liquid like something from 'The X Files' was a different thing altogether.**

Spinach juice turned out to be one of the most pleasant surprises to come gushing from my juicer's spout since that first Cox's apple juice. Grassy, vibrant and clean-tasting. There was also a distinct taste of young, green hazelnuts to it, the sort we find in the shops in early autumn, still sporting their frilly leaves. Kids seem to love this juice, probably because of its poisonous green colour.

Spinach is high in oxalic acid, the stuff that makes your teeth feel furry and, more importantly, hinders the absorption of iron and calcium into our bodies. Restraint is called for. But it is packed with beta-carotene and folic acid, which is necessary for building red blood cells and in which many of us are apparently deficient. We should also expect good amounts of trace elements such as magnesium and phosphorus.

Floppy leaves show signs of age and should be relegated to the compost. Juice only the lush and the squeakily fresh. No need to take off their stalks. But grit and sand, easily trapped in the leaves and between the stalks, should be scrupulously removed. Often a good rinse is not enough, and a quick soak (no more than a few minutes) in ice-cold water is the answer. Then wrap the leaves up in a plastic bag and stuff them into the fridge for an hour. In that time they will crisp up somewhat. Shove them slowly and not too tightly packed into the juicer. You will get a shot-glass worth of concentrated green liquor from each fat handful of leaves.

2 medium-sized green apples
2 large handfuls of spinach leaves
Spinach and Apple
Makes 1 medium glass

4 large, hard carrots
2 large handfuls of spinach leaves
Spinach and Carrot
Makes 1 medium glass

A green-tasting, nutty, refreshing juice. Dilute the spinach juice with sweet apple in the ratio of two big handfuls of leaves to two medium apples. A medium-sized glass is enough for anyone. Add both ingredients together so as not to 'choke' the juicer with a fat wad of leaves.

Remove the stalks from the apples and cut them into pieces that will easily go through the juice extractor. Push the apples and leaves through the juicer in alternate batches.

I am aware I am getting into dangerous 'health-victim' territory here, but it is a fine combination – fresh, sweet and invigorating. A medium-sized glass is probably as much as anyone needs, so juice two handfuls of spinach and four large winter carrots. The colour is that of a freshly laid cow pat. Fortunately, it tastes rather better (well, I guess).

Cut the carrots into quarters and alternate them with the spinach leaves going through the juicer (leaves are very good at clogging the juicer).

4 tomatoes
4 small to medium carrots
2 handfuls of small, tender
spinach leaves
Spinach, Carrot and Tomato
Makes 1 large glass

**Not the prettiest of colours
here, unless you are into
army uniforms, but the
flavour is that of creamy,
new-mown grass and
summer fields. There is also
the point that this is one way
to take spinach that doesn't
have the effect of making
your teeth feel as if they are
made of rubber.**

**Push everything through
the juicer.**

Strawberry

Why juice a strawberry? I asked exactly that question the first time I pushed a punnet of them through the juicer. And then I ended up with a jewel-like nectar with the intense, almost heady essence of the fruit. It was as if I had discovered attar of strawberry, the very soul of the fruit. Too much, really, to drink as a straight juice, and anyway, it is difficult to justify crushing a box of perfect berries when you could eat them, one by one, dipped into thick, cold, yellow cream.

Where strawberry juice shines, and it

does truly shine, is as a mixer. You only need a little with, say, orange or peach to give a clear berry flavour. Even a small handful thrown in with the other fruit will perfume and sweeten.

Strawberries are around all year and, despite purist grumbles, winter berries are actually rather good. Yes, buy locally grown ones from late May to October, but don't automatically expect them to have a deeper flavour than those that have travelled from France or Spain. You can use the juicer or blender here. You need not remove the green leaves before you juice, unless you are whizzing the whole thing in the blender. If you use a blender you will end up with a thin purée, which can be thinned down even further, with minimal loss of flavour, using mineral water. Citrus juice of any sort brings out the flavour of the berries even more.

Strawberries contain rich levels of beta-carotene, vitamin C and vitamin A and small but worthwhile amounts of magnesium, phosphorus and potassium. They are supposed to be good for the liver. And, bless them, they are low in calories.

250g strawberries
the juice of 2 oranges
ice cubes

Strawberry and Orange Juice

Makes 1 medium to large glass

100ml (a tub-for-one) vanilla ice-cream
200g strawberries
200ml milk

Strawberry Milk Shake

Makes 2 medium glasses

Sometimes you make a discovery that is so stonkingly good, you can't understand why no one got there before you. Strawberry and orange juice is that discovery. Quite the most invigorating, dazzling and exciting juice you will ever come across. Eminently drinkable. This is one juice I serve over ice cubes.

Remove the green leaves from the strawberries if you wish – it doesn't make a lot of difference, the leaves have been used in a healing sense for centuries – then push them through the juicer. Top up the glass with the orange juice, then pour over ice.

There is nothing remotely healthy about this. But then I see nothing wrong with organic ice-cream, full cream milk and fresh strawberries from time to time. A velvety, vividly pink, rather camp drink. Creamy and deeply strawberry.

Let the ice-cream soften slightly so it does not strain the blender motor. Rinse and hull the berries, then put them in the blender with the ice-cream and milk. Blitz till thick and creamy.

2 small, ripe peaches
10 strawberries
mineral water
a small tub (about 100ml)
frozen yogurt
Strawberry–Peach Frozen Yogurt Drink
Makes 2 large glasses

a sweet, pink or ruby grapefruit
an orange
20 strawberries
Strawberry and Grapefruit
Makes 1 medium glass

If you have an obscenely ripe and heavily aromatic peach, don't even think of juicing it. Just eat it as it is, in all its glory. If, on the other hand, you have a good supply of reasonably priced fruit that are sound, ripe and in need of using, then juice them.

Ghastly name, but once the frothy, Seventies-pink drink hits your lips you won't care what I've called it. It tastes like melted strawberry-and-peach ice. Despite the berry colour, it is actually pretty peachy.

Cut the peaches in half, twist and pull out the stone. Slice them, and the strawberries, into a blender. Pour in a small glass of mineral water and add the slightly softened frozen yogurt. Blend, slowly at first – the blender tends to jump when the yogurt hits the blades.

What a female friend of mine calls a girly juice.

Cut the peel from the citrus fruits, but don't worry too much about the white pith. In a fruit salad it would be horrid but it is actually good for you, so it can go in here. Push the fruits, including the strawberries and their leaves, through the juicer.

2 medium-sized apples, sharp
and green
10–12 strawberries
Apple and Strawberry
Makes 1 medium glass

In the early summer, we
have a choice of only last
autumn's stored apples or
imports. Neither really
excites me, but I do continue
making juice with them. One
way to cheer them up is to
toss in a box of strawberries.
Suddenly your juice is alive
and better than anything
you can buy in a bottle.

Cut the apples into pieces that
will fit through the juicer,
removing the stalks. Push
through the juicer with the
strawberries – you can leave
their leaves on; I do. The
result will be a clear, ruby-red
juice, sweet but not cloying,
and light on the stomach.

Tomato **Forget the dark scarlet juice from tins, bottles and Tetrapacks. Fresh tomato juice is a different thing altogether. At first, it seems insipid, a pale imitation of the 'real thing'. Then it hits you that this is the real thing; at once clean and fresh-tasting, as pure as biting into a plump, vine-ripened tomato itself. After a few glasses of this you will link commercial tomato juice with tomato purée rather than the fresh fruit itself (even so, don't even think of making a Bloody Mary with fresh juice; it will look watery and disappoint everyone). The colour is a bit of a letdown – a sort of salmon pink, even from the ripest, sweetest tomatoes – and the texture is somewhat grainy. It is, though, a supremely good mixing juice,** especially with greens such as watercress, cucumber and celery.

A tomato loses much of its point when pushed through a juicer. Gone that fragrant jelly flesh and slippery seeds, no more that herbal smell of freshly picked fruit. What you end up with is a small glass of pink slush. But that slush is full of lycopene, a powerful antioxidant that is linked with preventing cancers, especially the male variety. There's more, too: tomato juice is renowned as a great cleanser, while the fruits themselves have few calories and carry a fair bit of beta-carotene.

It is not difficult to find decent tomatoes nowadays, even in winter, but I still think that the best-flavoured fruits are those grown on home territory. Those late-season ones that appear in July, August and right on until the frosts seem to have the best flavour – by which I mean that deep sweet-tartness. Best of all is when tomatoes are mixed with red peppers; you get a glass of the most vibrantly flavoured juice imaginable – a great lazy weekend drink.

5 tomatoes
3 small to medium carrots
a few basil leaves
a little salt
Tomato and Carrot
Makes 1 large glass

4 tomatoes
2 large stalks of celery
5 radishes
a handful of parsley
Tomato, Celery, Parsley and Radish
Makes 1 large glass

87

A light juice, choc-a-bloc with vitamin C, beta-carotene and, of course, that lycopene I mention above. It is inclined to be a bit frothy and bubbly, but just drink it down and think of all those antioxidants. Kids are happy to drink this one, by the way, especially if they have made it themselves.

Make sure everything is cold from the fridge. Slice the tomatoes into quarters, halve the carrots, then push all through the juicer. Season with a little salt.

88

Of all the drinks in this book, this is probably the one with the dodgiest colour. Somehow, those brilliant reds and greens end up the shade of a pair of tights. Never mind, all that matters in this case is that it has a clean, fresh taste of tomato (none of the pizza flavour of the bottled stuff) and it is as good a detox juice as you will find, cleansing quietly and effectively. The radishes give it a bit of a lift. It is a great one for a hangover. If, that is, you can manage a large glass of beige-coloured liquid the morning after.

Blitz.

2 red peppers
4 tomatoes
a small piece of red chilli or
one bird's eye chilli
Worcestershire sauce, salt,
black pepper, Tabasco

Sunday Morning Tomato Crush

Makes 1 medium glass

I don't want to nominate favourites, but this is possibly my favourite vegetable juice in the book. It wins hands down on colour – a vibrant scarlet – and is rich and sweet in the mouth. The inclusion of raw red peppers might sound warning bells, but pushing them through a juice extractor has much the same effect as roasting them, in that it enhances their sweetness and deepens their flavour.

I always put the chilli in, but sometimes a shake of Tabasco and Worcestershire sauce too – normally on a Sunday morning, when lunch is already roasting in the oven and the kitchen is scattered with newspapers.

Cut the peppers in half and pull out the seeds and stalk. Rinse and cut into strips. Cut the tomatoes into chunks. Push the peppers, tomatoes and chilli through the juicer. Add seasonings to taste. I use a few shakes of Worcestershire sauce, salt, pepper and sometimes a bit of Tabasco.

Iced Cappuccino
Iced Mocha
Double Chocolate Milk Shake
Real Hot Chocolate
Hot Mocha with Gingernuts
Blueberry Banana Smoothie
Passion Fruit Ice-Cream
Smoothie
Clementine and Lemon Fizz
Bloody Mary

Indulgence

Thirst isn't, of course, just about gulping down a long, ice-cold drink to quench a deep fire. It's about warming, soothing and cocooning ourselves, too. Creamy, chocolatey drinks go a long way in terms of cosseting, as do long milky drinks such as thick, ice-cream-based shakes. These are not, perhaps, drinks for every day. These are no-holds-barred recipes for those times when we are in need of some serious comfort. I think of them as the adult equivalent of sucking my thumb.

2 cups of freshly made, really
strong espresso
2 balls of vanilla ice-cream,
or a 100ml tub
2 ice cubes
a little milk

Iced Cappuccino

Makes 1 large glass

Most of the iced coffees sold
in the American-owned
high-street coffee shops are
quite disgusting. Pale, thin
and oversweet is the best I
can say about them. The real
thing, made with ice-cream
and strong espresso, is on
another level altogether. It
is rather like melted coffee
ice-cream, though not quite
so high in fat. Forget the
commercial ones, make a
real one – rich, creamy, ice-
cold and with a massive
back-hit of coffee.

Pour the coffee into a
blender. Add the ice-cream
and ice cubes, then pour in
enough milk to blitz to a
thick, cool drink. I suggest
just a few drops of milk at
first. The consistency is up
to you – the less milk you
add, the thicker your
smoothie will be – but even
the smallest amount of milk
will thin it significantly. Add
sugar if you need to.

2 cups of freshly made, very
strong espresso
2 balls of chocolate ice-cream
2 ice cubes
a little milk

Iced Mocha

Makes 1 large glass

The marriage of coffee and chocolate is one made in heaven. Whoever thought of it gets my eternal admiration. I can't get enough of it, especially when the two flavours come together in an old-fashioned, village-fête type of cake. This drink comes in a close second.

Stick it all in a blender and whiz until smooth and frothy.

40g dark chocolate
2 balls of really good
chocolate ice-cream, such as
Green and Black's Organic or
Rocombe Farm
200ml cold milk
Double Chocolate Milk Shake
Makes 1 large glass

**Made with the finest
chocolate ice-cream and ice-
cold milk, this must be one
of the most luxurious drinks
on earth. I make it in a
rather unusual way, with
melted chocolate and
chocolate ice-cream, but it
is without doubt the best
chocolate milk shake ever.
Oh, and I know it sounds a
bit camp, but you really will
need a straw for this. It
won't feel right without one.**

**Break the chocolate into
small chunks and put it in
a small bowl sitting in, or
over, a small pan of gently
simmering water. Don't stir
it, but gently check that it
has melted – it shouldn't
take more than a couple
of minutes.**

**Drop the ice-cream into a
blender, then pour in half the
milk. Mix the other half into
the melted chocolate, then
pour it into the blender. Blitz
till all is dark and frothy.**

100g dark, fine-quality
chocolate
400ml milk
Real Hot Chocolate
Enough for 2

This is the most soothing, satisfying, glorious hot chocolate in the world. Much depends on the type of chocolate you use. Anything with less than 60 per cent cocoa solids (the content is marked on the wrapper) is likely to fail to ring your bell. You may need a little sugar in it, but taste it first.

Break the chocolate into small pieces. Put it into a small basin balanced over a saucepan of gently simmering water. Leave it to melt, but avoid the temptation to stir and fiddle. Bring the milk to the boil in a milk pan, remove the chocolate from the heat and pour a little of the milk into it. Stir until you have a thick paste, then pour over the rest of the milk, whisking as you go. You will end up with a big, frothy bowl of chocolate.

A few things to dunk in your hot chocolate:

HobNobs and Digestives
Mini doughnuts
Those pink wafers in biscuit assortments that no one else wants to eat
Croissants
Mini marshmallows

400ml milk (about 2 teacups)
2 level tablespoons ground
coffee
50g fine, dark chocolate,
chopped
sugar to taste
a packet of Gingernuts (well,
maybe not the whole packet)
Hot Mocha with Gingernuts
Enough for 4 small cups

Arriving home in deepest winter, cold through to my bones and virtually asleep on my feet, I sometimes make this drink. The milk soothes, the coffee lifts the eyelids, the chocolate seduces. It's rich, of course, too rich to drink in large amounts. You'll want no more than the smallest cup. But you will need some biscuits to dunk in it. Gingernuts would be stunning, but I wouldn't say no to a HobNob either.

Warm the milk in a small saucepan with the coffee and chocolate, stirring whilst it edges towards the boil. Put a little sugar into each cup and pour the mocha in through a tea strainer or small sieve (you can't do it without; the grounds make it sludgy). Drink while it is still piping hot, dunking the biscuits as you go.

2 handfuls (or a small
punnet) blueberries
250ml natural yogurt
2 bananas
a little milk to mix
2 ice-cubes
Blueberry Banana Smoothie
Makes 2 medium glasses

This is one those drinks that was born to be drunk on a Sunday morning, and has the ability to gently coax you back into the land of the living. (It is the exact opposite of the loud-alarm-clock effect of a glass of grapefruit juice.) Make it with raspberries or blackberries instead, if that is what you have. Either way, it is a deep, creamy meal-in-a glass.

Wash the berries and put them in the jug of a blender with the yogurt, the peeled bananas, the ice cubes and enough milk to thin it to a drinkable consistency.

Blitz.

4 passion fruit (large, heavy
for their size, and quite
wrinkled)
5 tablespoons natural yogurt
100ml vanilla ice-cream, plus
an extra scoop

**Passion Fruit Ice-Cream
Smoothie**

Enough for one

Sometimes drinks stand on
the borderline between juice
and dessert. This is just such
a recipe, which is why it has
ended up in this chapter.
OK, you have the juice of 4
passion fruit and a hefty
addition of yogurt (which, it
goes without saying, will be
the unsweetened, organic
sort), yet you would be
pushing it to suggest that
this is anything more than
a sort of ice-cream float.
Hence its presence in the
sin-bin section.

Cut the passion fruit in half.
Balance a tea strainer or
small sieve over a small
bowl and scrape the seeds,
juice and flesh from the
passion fruit into it. Push
the juice and pulp (there
won't be much) through the
sieve with a teaspoon.
Pour the juice into a blender
and add the yogurt and
100ml ice-cream. Blitz till
creamy. Place a scoop of ice-
cream in the centre of a
wide, shallow glass or cup
and pour the drink over it.
Eat with a teaspoon.

2 balls of lemon sorbet, such
as Rocombe Farm's Lemon
spring water
6 clementines
Clementine and Lemon Fizz
Makes 1 medium glass

4 measures of vodka
a good glug of dry sherry
500–700ml tomato juice –
tinned or bottled, not freshly
juiced
a few shakes of
Worcestershire sauce
a few shakes of Tabasco sauce
several shakes of celery salt
a lime
2 short celery stalks, leaves
intact
Bloody Mary
Enough for 2, with seconds

97

It might seem inappropriate
to include this in the
Indulgence section. OK, so
it is here by default, but at
about 3 a.m. on a sweaty
summer's night this is the
drink I want. You simply tip
the sorbet into a blender and
squirt in the juice of several
small, sweet-sharp citrus
fruits. It is rather like
drinking a melted ice lolly,
but with a huge dose of
sparkle and fizz.

Put the sorbet into a
blender, halve and squeeze
the citrus fruits into it, then
blitz till frothy.

98

Sunday morning, the papers,
a big jug of spicy Bloody
Mary. You'll need a jug and
lots of ice cubes.

Half fill a jug with ice-cubes.
Pour in the vodka, sherry and
tomato juice. Season with the
Worcestershire sauce,
Tabasco and a few shakes of
celery salt. Squeeze just a
little lime juice over and stir.
Stick a short stalk of celery
into each glass.

Big thanks to –
Louise Haines and all at 4th Estate, Araminta Whitley and everyone at LAW, Rosemary Scoular and all at PFD, Nung Puinongpho. Simon Browning, Sean Perkins, Jeremy Coysten and Nicole Udry at North. Also to Edie Baker, Eleanor Dowsing, Verity Spragge, Frances Spragge, Charlotte Moore, Tony Moore, Kate Rogers, John Ward, Mrs. J. Parsonage, David Deme and everyone at Chegworth Farm, Kent, Tim Cook at Luckett Farm, Kent, Peter and Joan Clarke, Kingcup Farm, Buckinghamshire, Penny Hammond at Saltram House, Everyone at The Eden Project, Garry Greenland at Total Organics, Borough Market, Turnips at Borough Market, Alan Baker & Louise Cantrill, Lubna Chowdhary, Nick Higgins, Dianne & Tony Moore, John & Valerie Neale and John Bowers & Petra Lay.

First published in Great Britain in 2002 by Fourth Estate
A Division of HarperCollins Publishers
77–85 Fulham Palace Road, London W6 8JB
www.4thestate.com

10 9 8 7 6 5 4 3 2 1

A catalogue record for this book is available from the British Library

ISBN 1-84115-768-6

Interior Designed by North
Colour origination by Saxon Photolitho
Printed in Great Britain by Bath Press, Glasgow